CARGO AIRLINES

CARGO AIRLINES

Oliver Scharschmidt

cargolux

City of Luxembourg

Airlife
England

Introduction

Cargo Airlines is a selection from several thousand transparencies photographed by the author since the late 1980s. Portrayed are international carriers operating their dedicated full-freighter and combi-aircraft to and from Europe's commercial centres of London, Frankfurt, Amsterdam and Paris. To complement the Megacarriers, a network of international airports throughout Europe offers a cargo infrastructure to feed the capacity of scheduled passenger aircraft, the hub-and-spoke systems of overnight express freight companies, the independent niche market operators and small cargo airlines. Many of the aircraft are caught in action-shots with a caption describing the moment with further details, while a separate text tells the corporate history.

Oliver Scharschmidt
Viernheim, Germany

Acknowledgements

Thanks to Steffen Remmel and Michael Geis for putting their aviation literature at my disposal; to Matthias Winkler for supplying vital information on the histories of Antonov and Ilyushin freighters; to Michael Burbach for his help concerning North American fleets; to Herome Krier and Serge Braun for their information on rare visitors to Luxembourg airport, and to Patrick DeBlock for his continuous newsletters and reliable in-depth information on Ostend's B-707 and DC-8 freighter scene throughout the years. Special thanks to Martin Krause for proving a valuable companion on numerous travels within Europe, sharing the pure fascination in the photography of civil air transport through thick and thin. I am also grateful to many airlines for their written response to this project. I derived inspiration from a look behind the exciting scenes of the aircargo business on board several freighters arranged by Bertram Pohl, President of Cargo Lion.

Copyright © 1997 Oliver Scharschmidt

All photographs taken by the author.

First published in the UK in 1997
by Airlife Publishing Ltd

British Library Cataloguing in Publication Data
A catalogue record for this book
is available from the British Library

ISBN 1 85310 716 6

Typeset by Livesey Ltd, Shrewsbury

Printed in Hong Kong

Airlife Publishing Ltd

101 Longden Road, Shrewsbury SY3 9EB, England

AIR CANADA

Formed in 1937 as Trans Canada Air Lines, Lockheed L-10A twin-engined props soon started to fly regularly on the Vancouver–Seattle route as the company's first international service. During WWII, Lancastrians carried out transatlantic mail and transport flights to the UK, supporting the Canadian Armed Forces in Europe. During the 1950s Canada experienced an immigration wave, which demanded an adjustment of the fleet's capabilities in order to cater for the increasing traffic figures on the international passenger and cargo sectors, handled by DC-4M North Stars and L-1049 Super Constellations out of Toronto via Gander into an extending European network. During the 1960s more than forty Douglas DC-8 aircraft series 40 through 60 were accumulated, including the world's first DC-8-54F freighter in 1963. B-747-133s, L-1011 TriStars and the first new B-747-233B Combi from the line were taken into long-range service during the 1970s, joined by B-767-233s in the following decade. Air Canada was privatised during 1989, ordering thirty-four of the European Airbus A320-211s to replace the B-727s. Since its participation in Continental Airlines, an alliance agreement was signed with Air France in 1993. While ten, fifty-seat Canadair Regional Jets supported the home manufacturing market, Airbus Industrie received further orders from Montreal for six A340-313s and twenty-five A319-100s, which are having to share the Canadian skies with six Boeing B-767-333ERs during the last years of the century. During the mid-1990s, Air Canada's network included 120 airports in twenty-one countries, in North America, the Caribbean, Europe, India and the Middle East.

Approaching Zürich's Kloten Airport in summer 1987 is C-FTIU, Air Canada's DC-8-63AF all-freight version, arriving on a weekly cargo service from Toronto and Montreal via Prestwick, Scotland. This aircraft was the youngest of a dozen DC-8-63s to be phased into passenger service with Air Canada between 1960 and 70. C-FTIU was also the last of seven aircraft to be converted into a 63AF version during 1986, at a time when the other six Air Canada Super Sixty freighters had already been upgraded into the 73CF variant in 1984, promising a comparative fuel saving rate of sixteen per cent with its new engines. Evergreen International operated the 63AF as N818EV since late 1988, until it was sold to the much bigger Douglas fleet park of Airborne Express, Ohio, USA as N811AX in 1990, still active during 1995. Serving London and Frankfurt since the early 1980s, Air Canada Express moved its operations to Brussels in late 1984. Ten years later, in 1994, the European DC-8-73CF freight services were discontinued, with the aircraft being sold to DHL.

ACS OF CANADA

With its headquarters at Farnham, Quebec, Air Charter Systems came into existence in late 1986 when the first used Douglas DC-8F-55, C-FDWW, arrived to be based at Montreal — Mirabel, commencing operations on a profile that was brilliantly expressed by the mother company's name, World Wide Air Charter Transport System Inc. Five weeks later, in January 1987, the second DC-8F-55, C-FCWW, joined while the third, C-FIWW, completed the fleet in September 1989. Taking advantage of a sound stock of Douglas spare parts and existing maintenance and support facilities at Montreal, ACS had chosen a place that housed many series of Air Canada DC-8s from 1960 until the early 1980s. The three times forty-five tons of payload were offered to ad hoc charter customers anywhere in the world, performed livestock shipments, or followed the demand of seasonal markets, as well as being contracted on scheduled cargo services for palletised freight by major airlines. After six years of active charter work, C-FCWW and C-FDWW were sold to a lessor, Kalitta American International Airways of Detroit, in late 1992 and early 1993. C-FIWW continued to operate until early 1995, when MK Airlines of England was eager to add the 1965 maple leaf Jet Trader to its DC-8F-55 fleet as 9G-MKF. The aircraft reached its thirtieth year of operation in a good condition. Staying in the cargo business with temporarily leased Douglas DC-8F aircraft during the mid-1990s, ACS of Canada's future plans include passenger charters with leased Boeing 747s.

Parked at Ostend in May 1992 was C-FCWW, one of three ACS DC-8F-55s, after arrival from a chartered transatlantic flight from Canada. C-FCWW had appeared in Europe before on contract charters for Iberia Cargo, as well as flying the international freight schedules of Ethiopian Airlines out of Addis Ababa. Delivered to Philippine Airlines in 1965, the aircraft was purchased by KLM Royal Dutch Airlines as PH-DCW *Gerard Mercator* two years later, until during the 1980s when it was used by Surinam Airways and Arrow Air before receiving a stylish brown livery with a kind of 'Speed-Maple Leaf' in 1987.

ANTONOV DESIGN BUREAU
– INTERNATIONAL CARGO TRANSPORTER

Established in 1989 as a division of the famous Ukrainian freight transport manufacturer and mother company Antonov Design Bureau, commercial operations were started under the same name and introduced to the western world by AirFoyle Ltd of Luton, England. They acted as a general sales agent, marketing the virtues of the short-range An-72, the mid-sized An-12 and the high-capacity profiles of their An-22 turboprop, An-124 Ruslan and An-225 Mriya turbofan models on the world's cargo charter markets. ADB's fleet of six An-124s was joined by the 600-ton-class Mriya 'Dream' prototype, which took off for the first time in December 1988. A new niche in the market had been created and filled by these unique freighters, gradually developed by initial ad hoc charter operations for the UN, and they were gladly accepted by a growing number of fast-cycle industrial manufacturers running global production systems. Gaining experience with increasingly new tasks of transportation, ADB strived to attain its own operating licence during the mid-1990s, while AirFoyle, UK, still provided its invaluable marketing experience.

During spring 1991, Luxembourg Airport was a venue for the heavies of the Antonov Design Bureau, when CCCP-82027 was one of three Antonov 124s for which AirFoyle arranged to fly charters to the Gulf and in Asia on behalf of the Grand Duchy's Cargolux. At the time the picture below was taken, the 1988 Kiev-manufactured Ruslan still flew without a civil type certification. Bearing the USSR's red flag and the blue cheatline of the once largest airline of the world, and also the Union Jack painted overhead the AirFoyle titles, the aircraft caused quite a sensation.

Three Antonov 22 Anteis, the world's largest turboprop transport, were operated by the commercial division of the Antonov Design Bureau during 1995. While sixty-eight aircraft were produced since 1965, UR-09307 was one of the last to be rolled out in 1974, the year before the shutdown of the line at Tashkent, entering services with ADB in September 1994. Having picked up a charter contract of the aerospace industry, the freighter with four-bladed contrarotating propellers, each of 15,000 hp, was assigned to carry outsized Ariane rocket segments to Kourou in French Guyana in the 4.5m wide and high, and 33m long cargo compartment. Capable of hauling a maximum payload of eighty tons over 5,000 km, the 250-ton aircraft was designed to support the exploration of mineral deposits in Siberia, and to serve as a strategic troop and freight transporter.

AEROFLOT

First established as Dobrolet in 1923, the name Aeroflot appeared in 1932 on the increasing numbers of Antonov and Tupolev aircraft operating within eleven regional directorates. First international destination was Prague in 1937, followed by Stockholm and Sofia before the beginning of World War II. The Tupolev Tu-104 turbojet airliner entered international service to European capitals in late 1956, three years before the first of the successful Il-18 turboprop series showed up on the schedules. Aeroflot owned an approximate fleet of 4,000 to 5,000 fixed-wing aircraft and several thousands of helicopters, about 2,500 aircraft operated out of thirty-one directorates to 3,600 domestic destinations and to 117 cities in ninety-four countries. In a mutual agreement with Pan American World Airways in 1988, B-747 passenger flights were carried out between the Soviet capital and

New York–JFK, followed by Il-76 cargo flights via Amsterdam and Shannon in 1989. The end of the Soviet Union called for a restructuring process that created Aeroflot – Russian International Airlines since 1992 – introducing a new livery on five Airbus A310-308s. The joint stock company painted the new Russian flag on a reduced fleet of 129 aircraft, including five new PS90-powered Il-96-300s and a couple of leased B-767-300ERs since 1994 when 3.1 million passengers were flown worldwide to 130 countries, compared with a total of more than 100 million travellers ten years earlier. The dedicated freighter fleet of the mid-1990s mainly consisted out of Il-76TDs, with a minor complement of four new Tu-204C medium rangers, a couple of An-124-100s and a leased DC-10-30F.

Keeping its four Soloviev D-30KP engines on idle for a moment on Luxembourg's runway 26 in March 1994, the flight deck's crew of five was preparing for take-off in their Aeroflot Ilyushin 76TD, RA-76479. As one of sixteen Il-76TDs of Aeroflot, Russian International Airlines, the aircraft was one of more than 300 Il-76 series in service with civil operators at that time. Ten years earlier in 1985, RA-76479 was rolled out at Tashkent. The Il-76T version was introduced into Aeroflot in 1976 and started international cargo flights to Japan in 1978. Replacing the An-22 turboprops, the virtually self-handling and all-round work horse became the mainstay of Aeroflot's industrial logistics concept to Siberia and for worldwide cargo shipments. A future modernisation programme plans to install the Perm PS-90 engine in the fleet's sixteen Ilyushin 76TD and two Il-76Ts, and to acquire the Il-76MF version, stretched by 6.3 metres and capable of carrying a fifty-ton payload.

L'AÉROPOSTALE

Compagnie Générale Aéropostale was famous for the transportation of mail between 'Le Grande Nation' and the northern and western part of Africa in 1927. It also pioneered the route across the South Atlantic to Buenos Aires and Santiago de Chile in 1930. The trading name disappeared when it merged with Air Union and finally with Air France in 1933. The name L'Aéropostale re-emerged in 1990 when ICS Inter Ciel Service, which was founded as Inter Cargo System in 1987, and TAT integrated their Boeing 737-200C convertibles to form a new French cargo and passenger airline. The initial fleet comprised fifteen Fokker F-27 500s which had been operated by Air France on behalf of La Poste for more than twenty years, since 1969. The turboprops were phased out in 1991, while the first former Aéromaritime/UTA passenger B-737-300 series arrived in France after modification work created the first side-cargo-door 'Quick-Change' convertible of this type. The operational profile can be clearly divided into day and night-time activities. Scheduled passenger and charter flights in the day are complemented by an extensive nightly mail and courier distribution system, connected to an intermodal co-ordinated air freight/truck transport system, providing fifty flights between ten destinations throughout France. A fleet of twenty Boeing jets includes eighteen B-737s and two B-727s. As the number one company on the French domestic freight market, L'Aéropostale operates the largest European cargo fleet of medium-range aircraft out of its base at Paris–Charles de Gaulle. A feasibility study on Airbus A310/300 QC widebody operations evaluated the use of widebody quick-change aircraft during the mid-1990s, aiming to lead L'Aéropostale into the next century.

Rolling its way from Terminal Aérogare 2 at Paris–Roissy to the northern take-off runway of Airport Charles de Gaulle in June 1994, F-GIXF performs one of its roles as a passenger airliner on the networks of Air Inter, Air France, TAT or Air Charter. After midnight, the Boeing 737-300 (QC) will 'quick-change' into a freighter, a task that is completed in fewer than twenty minutes. Once the seats have gone, a maximum payload of eighteen tons of mail and magazines fills the available space for an early daytime delivery service between Paris and the main points at Nantes, Strasbourg, Lyon, Marseille, Mulhouse, Bordeaux and Toulouse.

AER TURAS TEORANTA – IRISH CARGO AIRLINES

Founded in 1962, Aer Turas started to fly with a single DH 89A Dragon Rapide biplane as a small operator of passenger and cargo charters out of its base at Dublin Airport. Douglas DC-4s, a Bristol 170 and a A.W. 650 Argosy, as well as Bristol Britannias and CL-44Js successively formed the airline's profile. In August 1980, Aer Lingus acquired a majority shareholding in Aer Turas, and cargo operations were then carried out on behalf of its mother company. Significantly boosting the company's cargo capacity and transportation speed came the new Douglas DC-8-63CF (later EI-BNA) flagship, on lease from Cargolux since late 1982. The freighter was purchased in 1984 and entered a long-lasting contract with SAUDIA, Saudi Arabian Airlines, in 1989, busily flying on their frequent cargo schedules out of Jeddah, Riyadh and Dharan to Brussels, as well as to Addis Ababa and Khartoum. The CL-44J was exchanged for another of the same type in 1986 (EI-BRP) and was sold to Heavylift Cargo Airlines three and a half years later in May 1989. This was the end of the turboprop era for Aer Turas, and two further Douglas DC-8-63F Super Sixty series (EI-CGO and EI-CAK) began operating worldwide charters with a special emphasis on livestock. EI-CAK was sold to Aerolease of Miami in late 1994 and continues to fly for the Detroit-based Air Transport International, while EI-BNA still shuttles between the Kingdom of Saudi Arabia and Brussels in the colours of SAUDIA. EI-CGO remained the only aircraft on the scene, displaying the green Irish clover leaf all over the world.

The sonorous sound of the last European-based 'Whispering Giant' of Aer Turas radiated across the field of Milan–Malpensa in summer 1987, when four Rolls-Royce Tyne 515/10 turboprop engines gently pushed the Canadair CL-44J, EI-BRP, to its take-off position for a northbound cargo return flight to Dublin. While twelve CL-44-6 military versions were ordered as 'Yukon' from the Royal Canadian Air Force as a derivative model of the Bristol Britannia, the pictured aircraft belonged to twenty-seven Canadian-manufactured CL-44-D4 versions, produced for the intercontinental commercial passenger and cargo market between 1961 and 1965. After nearly two years in service with Loftleidir on scheduled transatlantic flights with 189 passengers on board, the Icelandic operator's demands for larger capacity were realised by stretching the existing fuselage by 4.6m. Only four aircraft were converted into the larger CL-44J model, which could accommodate 214 passengers or handle a maximum payload of twenty-seven tons in the freighter configuration over a distance of approximately 4,020 km. EI-BRP was heavily used for livestock transport and flew services for Aer Turas from January 1986 until May 1989 as the company's second and last CL-44J.

AIR FRANCE

August 1933 saw the merging of aviation companies from the French pioneering days to create one of the world's largest airline route networks out of France. After World War II, in early 1946, Société Nationale Air France became the national and government-owned carrier, introducing a fleet of Douglas DC-3s, DC-4s and Lockheed L-1049 piston liners. During 1959, the legendary Sud Aviation Caravelle was the first jet aircraft to be implemented in large numbers on short-haul routes, as well as on European schedules. Air France was the first customer of the Boeing 707-320, introducing twenty B-707-328s between January 1960 and 1962 to form the backbone of the intercontinental fleet. Between 1967 and 1968 the cargo branch was developed with the addition of seven convertible passenger/cargo B-707-328Cs. Air France was the first airline to use the short to medium-range widebody capacity Airbus A300B2 and B4 series, of which eighteen have entered service since 1974 (until 1982). As the largest Airbus customer worldwide, the 1,000th European aircraft was delivered to Air France in 1993, upgrading the intercontinental fleet with the first of a dozen sophisticated A340-311s. With ninety-eight per cent of Air France held by the government in 1995, a rehabilitation plan was executed prior to its privatisation, to be initiated in 1997 and coinciding with the complete deregulation of air traffic in the European market.

Rotating during take-off for an all-cargo schedule from Paris–Orly to Djibouti on the Red Sea and then on to Reunion in the Indian Ocean in 1992, is F-BPVR, part of Air France Cargo's ten B-747-200F-strong dedicated 'Super Pelican' freighter fleet. With the first B-747-228F (SCD) inaugurated in late 1974, F-BPVR followed as the second aircraft two years later in 1976, using CF6-50E engines instead of the Pratt & Whitney JTD9D-7s. The B-747-228Fs of Air France Cargo were loaded with a practical long-range payload of ninety-four tons, cruising at a speed of 600 mph, or 965 km per hour. The total fleet of forty-five B-747s of the mid-1990s comprised ten full freighters and seventeen combi versions of the 200B (SCD), 300B (SCD/SUD) and 400B (SCD) series.

AIR HONG KONG

Air Hong Kong was established in 1986, and operates out of Kai Tak International Airport. Its first aircraft was VR-HKK, a former BOAC Boeing 707-336C that was initially bought and then later leased. A second, ex-Pan Am B-707-321C, VR-HKL, arrived from the lessor in May 1989, with both aircraft entering scheduled cargo services between Hong Kong, the UK and Japan in October 1989, as well as expanding the carrier's charter activities throughout the Asian region. Soon it became obvious that the B-707s, whose ages had already reached the early twenties, had to be replaced by more fuel-efficient high-capacity freighters on the long-haul distances. VR-HKN/M had already been converted into full-fledged B-747-132F freighters by Boeing at Wichita in 1977, equipped with all the necessary internal and external features such as a strengthened floor, cargo handling systems, and a hinged front - as well as a side-cargo door. The widebodies started to fly extensive European services via Dubai in the Gulf to Manchester on five days of the week, continuing their routings to Brussels, from where the freighters returned to south-east Asia. A third B-747-132F, VR-HKC was operated temporarily on lease during 1993, while in 1994 a -132F was exchanged for a first 249F series with greater range and a higher payload capacity. In May 1994, Cathay Pacific Airlines Cargo acquired a seventy-five per cent shareholding in Air Hong Kong. In early 1996, mother company Cathay Pacific announced the leasing of three ex-VARIG Boeing 747-2L5B Combis from a Bermuda-based lessor, after the aircraft's final conversions into full freighters were completed by Hong Kong's HAECO maintenance company; these aircraft were to replace Air Hong Kong's two remaining B-747-132F and 249F freighters on lease from Polaris until 1996/97.

Arriving at Brussels as 'Air Hong Kong One' on the six-times-a-week trunk route to Europe during August 1992, is the company's first Boeing 747-132F, VR-HKN, completing its voyage having made stops at Dubai and Manchester. Once belonging to the early 1970 fleet of five Delta Air Line's passenger jumbos, the converted aircraft's career as a freighter started in 1977 when operated by the Flying Tiger Line, El Al, and later by Federal Express throughout the 1980s until summer 1991, when Air Hong Kong took over the handsomely coloured aircraft.

AIR ATLANTIQUE / ATLANTIC AIR TRANSPORT

Founded as an air-taxi company in September 1969 by the Jersey-based General Aviation Services Ltd, a fleet of Douglas DC-3 Dakotas commenced cargo and later passenger charter services under the name of Air Atlantique in 1977, linking the largest of the Channel Islands with destinations throughout England and continental Europe, including flights as far as Africa and the Middle East. Owners of the largest European fleet of commercial DC-3s, cargo operations of up to six Douglas freighters were regrouped and moved to London–Stansted under the name of Atlantic Air Transport in 1983, while two Dakotas remained based at Jersey carrying out air-taxi and passenger charters, corporate hospitality and airshow pleasure flights. In 1986 Coventry Airport was selected as Atlantic Air Transport's new corporate headquarters and maintenance base. Welcomed to the fleet in 1987 were two Douglas DC-6 freighters; the company owned G-SIXC and G-APSA. During the early 1990s, the Atlantic Group created new divisions out of Atlantic Air Transport at Coventry. The first was Atlantic Airways in 1991, offering a wide range of passenger aircraft for charter or lease. In the same year Atlantic Cargo followed, offering a quick-response service aimed at the parcel integration market, ad hoc charterers and other airlines in need of capacity between 2,200 and 14,500kg. For that purpose, three Lockheed L-188CF/AF Electras were introduced for the upper end of the company's payload scale, flying actively on DHL night-time sectors throughout Europe, as well as for manufacturers of the automotive industry and other customers. A twenty-two-ton capacity Lockheed L-100-30 Hercules (ZS-RSI) was leased from Safair in early 1995, the flight logs of the South African crews being filled with European mission reports, but also including such interesting assignments as flying support to the remote motor-rally team camps in the Rallye Granada–Dakar, in the heart of the Mauritanian desert.

G-SIXC, *Jimmy The One* at Brussels in May 1992. This DC-6A/B carries a payload of 13,000kg of palletized or bulk cargo. The freighter's intensive day-to-day work included nightly newspaper services and the haulage of car components. Its service life recorded operations for carriers in Taiwan, Kingdom of Laos, Southern Air Transport and Trans Continental Airlines in the USA as N93459.

AIR BRIDGE CARRIERS

Belonging to the Hunting Group, Air Bridge Carriers (ABC) was founded in November 1972 as a subsidiary of Field Aviation. It operated pure cargo charters out of its base at East Midlands Airport, England. High fuel prices during the late 1970s again favoured the economy of the Rolls-Royce Tyne 1 Mk 506 turboprop engines while five of a total of seven Vickers Merchantman 953Cs were purchased between the end of 1979 and January 1980. Extensive use was also made of Lockheed Electra L-188AF and CF versions, with several models bought and leased since 1988.

As a result of reorganization, the trading name Air Bridge Carriers was switched to Hunting Cargo Airlines during mid-August 1992. The Electra and the Boeing 727-200F were chosen to form the stronghold of the cargo fleet, with all aircraft receiving a completely new corporate identity.

G-APEP *Superb*, bearing the livery of Air Bridge Carriers at Amsterdam in May 1992. This Vickers 953C Merchantman freighter was one out of nine converted Vanguard 953 passenger aircraft previously belonging to British European Airways. Six models of the 951 series arrived from early 1959 until March 1960, and fourteen 953 series models with larger seat capacity and stronger R-R Tyne engines were taken into service between May 1961 and March 1962. G-APEP *Superb* became the world's last Merchantman cargo aircraft in operation during 1996.

AIR CHINA INTERNATIONAL

Established in 1949 as the Civil Aviation Administration of China, CAAC commenced operations with a fleet of Soviet-manufactured Lisunov Li-2s, built in Tashkent as licensed versions of the Douglas C-47. The first Western aircraft to be placed into the vast Chinese market were six Vickers Viscount 843 models in 1963/64, flying for CAAC for twenty years until being sold in 1983. It was not until 1970 that the jet age arrived in the form of a Trident 1E, purchased from Pakistan Airlines. This was followed by a large number of new Trident 2E deliveries. During the late 1970s, China pursued an opening-up process to form a socialist market economy, and resumed diplomatic relations with the USA, which became its second largest customer behind their big trader Hong Kong. China's population reached the billion mark during the early 1980s, a decade earmarked by tremendous expansion and purchases of a large variety of airplanes. Four Boeing 747SPs were chosen to move the masses across the Pacific from Shanghai to San Francisco, or via Sharjah to Europe, while five new McDonnell-Douglas MD-82s became based in the region in 1982; they also rolled off a domestically-licensed line five years later in 1987, manufactured by the Shanghai Aviation Industrial Corporation. Owning more than 160 aircraft during 1988, CAAC served ninety domestic and twenty-eight international destinations in twenty countries. During the summer of 1996, six decentralised and independent carriers were forged out of the existing monolithic network, restructuring regional CAAC administrations into autonomous companies. Air China International at Beijing was established to operate foreign as well as domestic services out of the capital. From then on, the freight department rapidly developed with the aquisition of a Boeing 747-4J6 combi in 1989, followed by two more in 1990, together with a B-747-2J6F all-cargo aircraft. The fleet of a dozen B-747s comprises six combi aircraft and a freighter, accounting for a total number of twenty-six widebodies on international routes, together with four B-747SPs and ten B767-200 and 300s, while the regional market is served by twenty-one B-737-200/300s and four BAe 146-100s.

Air China Cargo's sole B-747-2J6F freighter flagship, B-2462, has gained respectable ground over the threshold's end at Frankfurt on a weekly non-stop trans-Siberian cargo service to Beijing, on a hot day in July 1995. Delivered to Air China in late October 1990, the aircraft started to serve Los Angeles and several Asian destinations, until opening European routings via Dubai to Frankfurt and Copenhagen in 1991. Three B-747-200 combis served Hong Kong, Tokyo, Osaka, New York and Vancouver as well as Milan and Rome in Italy, while three of the B-747-400 combis linked China with San Francisco, Frankfurt and Paris–CDG.

AIR INDIA

Originating from the private Tata Airlines, first regular mail services were carried out under this trading name between Karachi and Madras in 1933, until operations were renamed Air India during 1946, using a number of Douglas DC-3s and Vickers Vikings. The company's first two B-747-237B widebodies arrived in spring 1971, counterbalancing the tremendous growth in passenger traffic on flights to the Persian Gulf, with tens of thousands of Indian people seeking their fortune during the oil-boom. Airbus widebodies started to take over the duties of the B-707-337Bs, with three medium-range A300B4-203s flying since 1982 and six A310-304s on long-range routes since 1987. Two Boeing 747-337 passenger/cargo combis were added to the network in 1988 and gradual expansion continued during the early 1990s with the purchase of two further A310-304s and three Boeing 747-437s. Two McDonnell-Douglas DC-8-73Fs of Miami-based Southern Air Transport were contracted in 1994 to carry out full-payload westbound cargo operations linking key Indian cargo points via the Middle East with Brussels and Zürich, as well as with New York–JFK.

Above:
Operated by Southern Air Transport/Miami, N875SJ's four CFM56-2C1 engines' reverse-thrust, powerfully streaming deflected fan air through fixed cascade vanes and blowing up the moisture from Ostend's freezing runway 08 on 22 December 1994. Newly delivered to Southern Air in late September 1994 and expanding the DC-8-73F fleet to three, the pictured aircraft was immediately placed into service as the second aircraft flying long-term contract charters for Air India Cargo. The shot shows N875SJ arriving at Ostend from Madras and Dubai to stay just for a short fuel-stop and to continue the weekly AI197 India–New York flight via Gander to JFK. The aircraft was an original DC-8-63 passenger version purchased by VIASA in May 1969. Re-engined into a DC-8-73 version during 1984, Europe became its new home and final place for long-haul passenger charters out of Paris–Orly for Minerve and later out of Copenhagen for Time Air Sweden, before becoming part of the straining duties of the cargo business as a converted freighter in the experienced hands of Southern Air in 1994.

Below:
With the upper-deck rear cargo compartment of VT-EPX being packed with pallets in summer 1990, Air India's second Boeing 747-347 was bringing in a regular consignment of textiles and handicrafts on five weekly combi services from Bombay and Delhi to Frankfurt, Europe's strongest cargo destination for Indian exports. The pictured VT-EPX appears in a livery that was introduced in late 1989 and then abandoned in favour of the legendary 'Maharajah' style from 1971.

AIR JET

Founded in May 1980 by the French Jet Services Group, passenger and freight charters were carried out under the name of Air Jet using a Fokker F-27 Friendship 400, F-GCJV, which was later complemented by a smaller but faster Beechcraft King Air executive turboprop. Scheduled passenger flights were maintained between Avignon and Lyon, while overnight parcel services were operated from its base at Paris–Orly to domestic points at Avignon, Lyon and Bordeaux. The second Friendship, a 600, followed in 1984 and the fleet totalled five side-cargo-door, quick-change convertibles until late 1989. Each could accommodate a maximum of forty-eight pallet-mounted seats, or carry light freight, such as packages, newspapers or light boxes on a normal cargo floor. The pure turboprop fleet was joined by a first BAe 146-200 QC (F-GLNI) in October 1991, the airline being an early European customer of this quick-change version. All five Friendships were sold to WDL Aviation of Cologne in early 1995. A third BAe 146-200QC was leased from British Aerospace in March 1996, while Paris–Charles de Gaulle became the new home of the pure jet fleet, serving Avignon, Strasbourg and Toulouse on overnight cargo services.

F-GHRC was the last of five Fokker F-27 Friendship 600s to join the fleet of Air Jet in late 1989. Here it waits for night-time at the Zone de Fret of Paris–Orly in June 1990 before flying parcel shipments to Avignon, Bordeaux and Lyon. Cruising at 480 kmh at 6,000m altitude and carrying a payload of up to six tons over 1,900 km, the F-27 600 was an efficient airplane in its class. The service life of this aircraft reflects the versatility of this pioneering Dutch turboprop, the F-27 prototype first flying in 1955. This aircraft was delivered to All Nippon Airways in 1964 as a basic 200 model; it then passed through service with Air Niugini and Aviateca in the mid-1970s. A freight door was added when being converted into a F-27 400M and enlarged passenger doors on both sides (to drop paratroopers) while flying for the Guatemalan Air Force during the 1980s. Fokker finally made a series 600 aircraft out of it in 1987 and leased it to Sudan Airways until it was purchased by Air Jet.

AIR SOFIA

A refreshing love for attractive detail must have inspired the founders of the young Bulgarian Air Sofia when in 1992 they decided to paint the propeller blades blue to contrast with the white fuselage. LZ-SFA was the ad hoc cargo charter company's first Antonov 12B freighter, which was taken over from the defunct Sofia-based carrier Sigi Air Cargo. It was the sole survivor of the civil version of a six-strong fleet of military variants produced before 1965, which included the pictured LZ-SFM. It is seen entering Ostend's runway 26 in May 1995. Air Sofia's seven An-12s were contracted by Turkish Airlines Cargo on flights from Istanbul to Basle, to Maastricht and to Stansted, with one freighter being held at the ready at Manston, Kent International Airport.

TIME AIR SWEDEN

This charter company, formed in 1991, operated inclusive-tour flights from their base in Stockholm to points in Europe, the Mediterranean and the Canary Islands using leased all-passenger Boeing 737-200 and 300 series aircraft. A Douglas DC-8-71 was leased from the GPA Group Ltd in December 1991, three months prior to delivery of the company's first all-cargo jet, SE-DLM, in March 1992. This aeroplane subsequently shuttled between Europe and India on a long-term charter contract. The traditionally strong Scandinavian passenger charter market reached a saturation point and eventually Time Air Sweden ran into financial difficulties and ceased operations in February 1993, returning all their aircraft to their lessors.

SE-DLM, Time Air Sweden's sole DC-8-71F dedicated freighter at Ostend, Belgium in August 1992. Named *Italian Rainbow*, the aircraft has just arrived from Stockholm on a weekly scheduled cargo charter operation. It will continue its routing with a technical stop at Dubai, before reaching its final destination at Bombay, India. During December 1992 the Air Sweden Cargo livery on the aircraft's left-hand side was repainted with Indian-type letters indicating Forbes Cargo as the charterer. Once a proud member of a fleet of thirty passenger DC-8-61s delivered to United Airlines in May 1968, the aircraft

experienced two technical modifications during its operational life. CFM56 engines were fitted in 1983, upgrading the aircraft into the 71 series. Already owned by GPA Group Ltd, modifications continued into late 1991 and finally the suffix 71'F' made a real freighter out of it, incorporating all the advanced features required for the cargo business. The aircraft now flies for the Californian Burlington Air Express. Climbing out in the background is a DC-8-55F of Liberia World Airlines, c/n 45683, which originally left the Douglas plant at Long Beach as a pure freighter in 1964.

ALITALIA

Contributing to the early days of aviation, Italian Savoia Marchetti flying-boats gained their reputation from flying across the South Atlantic in 1927. In November 1957 the present name Alitalia was adopted. On cargo routes, two DC-7CF freighters were operated together with five passenger sister-ships. Operating out of Rome–Ciampino, the jet age was welcomed with sixteen Rolls-Royce Conway R Co.12-powered Douglas DC-8-42s and 43s, intercontinental series, being routed to North and South America, Africa and via the Middle East to the Far East and Australia during the first five years of the 1960s. Most of the twenty-one new Sud Aviation Caravelles, all delivered up to 1966, started their schedules out of their new base at Rome–Fiumicino (FCO) in 1961, extending the network to eighty-one points in forty-nine countries. In 1972, two B-747-143s and three B-747-243s joined the DC-8-43s and DC-8-62Hs on intercontinental routes, with the

latter type being phased out by 1981. From late 1980 until 1986, five B-747-243 combis, six further all-passengers and one freighter were purchased; the initial five B-747-143s were returned to Boeing. Other aircraft to appear during the early 1980s were the widebody Airbus A300B3-203, the Boeing 727-243 and the McDonnell-Douglas MD-82, which was bound to form the core of the European operations in numbers of up to sixty aircraft during the mid-1990s, serving twenty-six domestic and thirty-seven European destinations, part of a total fleet of more than 130 aircraft. Eight MD-11s entered services between 1991 and 1994, while two B-767-33A(ER)s were leased from Ansett Worldwide Aviation Services in early 1995, employing non-union crews for operation. The stretched Airbus A321-112 180-seater was the newest model for the European network and its numbers are planned to be increased by a further twenty-two by 1998.

I-DEMC, named after the ancient Taormina at the foot of the Sicilian volcano Mount Etna, is about to land at Milan–Malpensa with the early morning sun of summer 1987 challenging the stylish timeless Italian livery of the early 1970s. The pictured aircraft was the first of five Boeing 747-243B combifreighters delivered in late 1980 to begin Alitalia's significant B-747 fleet expansion of twelve aircraft. The combis spent the most time in the air among the fleet's other B-747 models, flying a daily average of 11.4 hours, carrying 298 passengers and a total of thirty-eight tons of main-deck and lower-hold cargo. The all-passenger aircraft had a utilisation rate of 9.8 hours, and the 111-ton payload B-747-243F just seven hours. Dedicated B-747 freight services of the mid-1990s were mainly eastward bound, departing Rome via India to China or Japan. Scheduled cargo flights to Bahrain and Hong Kong, as well as to New York–JFK included Milan–Malpensa as an important loading stop.

Arriving at Milan–Malpensa in March 1992 as flight AZ620 from Rome on its first leg of the daily routing to Los Angeles, is Alitalia's first delivered McDonnell Douglas MD-11 combifreighter, I-DUPE, Arena di Verona, which entered the fleet in late November 1991. California is reached in twelve hours and twenty minutes, which is approximately the same flying time as the non-stop MD-11C service from Rome to Hong Kong. The longest MD-11 all-passenger routing out of Rome is Buenos Aires, with an inflight time of fourteen hours. Alitalia was the first customer to order the combi version, operating five of eight delivered aircraft during 1995 in a mixed configuration, accommodating 204 passengers and six 88 x 125 inch freight pallets in the aft compartment of the main-deck, or with 283 passengers enjoying their flight surrounded by an interior designed by Giorgio Armani. A distinctive feature of the combi is the freight door cut into the rear fuselage, while the MD-11F all-freighter and convertible freighter versions are loaded through a port-side forward cargo door.

ARROW AIR

During the early 1980s, a fleet of up to eight leased Boeing 707s, mostly 300C convertible freighters, was accumulated, together with a large number of Douglas DC-8 series 54F, 62CF and 63CF freighters, as well as passenger aircraft from the Super Sixty family, in the main DC-8-62s. Passenger charters were carried out on the former Air Florida routes from Miami to Europe, as well as cargo charters into the Caribbean, with regular cargo flights to San Juan and to New York–JFK. Scheduled passenger flights linked Montego Bay, Jamaica, with Denver, Los Angeles and San Francisco, as well as Denver and Tampa with London–Gatwick. In the aftermath of a DC-8-63PF's crash at Gander in late 1985, the FAA temporarily grounded Arrow Air's DC-8 fleet, followed by a period of Chapter 11 operations in early 1986. Introducing a couple of DC-8-62Fs to the fleet the same year, Arrow Air's expansion continued again, flying worldwide charter contracts for major airlines and scheduled cargo charters out of Miami throughout major Caribbean, South and Central American cities. During the mid-1990s, a mix of five B-727-200 freighters and passenger series provided cargo and charter services from points in the north-west, mid-west, south-east and Miami into Puerto Rico, and mainly throughout the Americas, while a large fleet of DC-8-62Fs and 63Fs specialised in perishable and time-sensitive shipments.

Arrow Air's DC-8-63CF freighter N661AV builds speed for a take-off from runway 18, Frankfurt, where it regularly operated on behalf of Lufthansa during the late 1980s. The two companies had an agreement that stipulated the onward distribution of Lufthansa's cargo to Central and South American points out of Arrow Air's headquarters in Miami. With the carrier's 'Big A' easily made out on the tail-fin, a small VIASA sticker on the upper aft fuselage indicates the freighter's previous chartered occupation on cargo routings of the major Venezuelan airline.

AIR TRANSPORT INTERNATIONAL

Air Transport International was created in 1989. The early 1990s saw a gradual enlargement of the pure McDonnell Douglas long-haul fleet, which grew with the introduction of four DC-8-63Fs in 1991/92. During 1994, ATI contracted to operate nine DC-8-71Fs of Toledo, Ohio-based Burlington Air Express on their scheduled freight services to more than thirty points in the United States. During 1994, ATI's fleet received two DC-8-63Fs and five DC-8-62Fs, of which four were operated on own-behalf and three were combi-freighters for a configuration of twenty-seven to thirty-two passengers and ten pallets. During the mid-1990s, ATI held twelve Douglas DC-8 freighters of the series 61F, 62F and 63F at the ready at Detroit–Willow Run, to respond to demands for chartered international, long-range freight work.

Douglas DC-8-63F(AF) N786AL Super Sixty series of Detroit-based Air Transport International, arriving from a non-scheduled transatlantic cargo charter in March 1995, to be unloaded at Schiphol–Oost. Twenty years before being converted into a full freighter during 1990, this aircraft proudly carried the blue colours of KLM Royal Dutch Airlines and was named *David Livingstone*. It was one of eleven DC-8-63s. Successively flying for Icelandair, ATI took over the freighter from Aer Turas, the Irish cargo airline, in 1994. More than 300 of a total of 556 manufactured DC-8s were still in service during 1993, while most of all 878 produced Boeing 707s had nearly vanished from the North American continent.

ATLAS AIR

This new, fast-growing, US-certificated B-747-200F freighter company from Golden, Colorado, arrived on the air freight scene in the early 1990s to meet the world trade's increasing demand for air freight capacity, offering long-haul and high gross weight cargo hauling for major airlines. Atlas Air leased its first B-747-200F in late 1992, followed by a single B-747-128F and a second B-747-200F in 1993, and the introduction of four converted Lufthansa passenger-combi aircraft in 1994. Through an alliance with major European banks, the financial staying power of Atlas Air provided a solid background to further increase the fleet of dedicated freighters. Company objectives were to offer a range of time-definite, scheduled or contract charters and sub-services for major airlines, offering worldwide flexible air cargo shipments on existing routes to consolidators and forwarders. Atlas Air considered the B-747-200F, with a capability of hauling 117 tons as far as 3,575 miles, as the ideal aircraft to grant high-performance, reliable and cost-effective services with more payload available than most other carriers could offer. A further six, former Thai Airways passenger B-747-2D7Bs were taken over during 1996 to be converted into freighters by Israel Aircraft Industries, and to be added to the existing fleet of eight freighters by 1998. Five former FedEx B-747-200Fs are also to join the expanding fleet. Atlas Air aims to have twenty B-747 freighters in operation by the year 2000 and to become a major player on the air cargo market. A future fleet development is planned to include DC-10-30CF freighters as well.

Correcting the course before flaring-in for an initial visit to Luxembourg in March 1993 is N505MC, the first side-cargo-door-equipped Boeing 747-2D3B freighter, newly leased from the Atlas Air Holding's sister company Aeronautics Leasing. All Captains flying the 'Giants' had at least 10,000 hours, or twenty years, of commercial flying experience, most of which was international. The pictured B-747 started its service life with ALIA, the Royal Jordanian Airline as JY-AFA *Prince Ali* during 1977, served the global networks of the French UTA and later Air France from 1989 until entering Atlas Air Holding in 1992.

TRANS AVIA EXPORT

Belorussia, the western part of the former USSR, was a foundation member of the CIS in 1991. As one of the oldest Russian cities, its capital Minsk housed 1.6 million inhabitants during the early 1990s, and was the country's centre of industrial production, specialising in mechanical engineering, metal processing and truck manufacturing. While national carrier Belavia operated a large passenger fleet of regional Yak-40 jets, Antonov 24 and 26 turboprops, as well as forty short-range Tupolev 134s and medium-range Tu-154s out of Loshitsa International Airport, Belorussia's main cargo lift capacity lay in the hands of the freighter pilots of Trans Avia Export. Founded in 1992, the first of sixteen Ilyushin 76MDs paid an inaugural visit to civil European airports in June 1993, contracted for a fortnight to fly German-produced pesticides daily out of Luxembourg to cotton producers in Kazakhstan. Like nearly all former states of the Warsaw Treaty, Belorussia joined the mutual rapprochement politics with NATO, as the fourth largest nuclear power of the CIS after Russia, Ukraine and Kazakhstan, signing a programme of Partnership and Freedom in January 1995 which included joint defence planning, humanitarian mission manoeuvres, and the exchange of military personnel. Staffed with skilfully trained and highly experienced flight crews, including good English-speaking captains, Trans Avia Export introduced its large airborne capacity to the Western freight charter scene in the early 1990s, eager to meet any challenge the transport market could throw at it – even the price war.

Flight 'Tango X-Ray Charley 006' softly touches down at Ostend in January 1994, arriving from Minsk, situated only 1,700 km to the east. EW-78848 was one of sixteen Ilyushin 76MDs of Belorussian cargo carrier Trans Avia Export. Manufactured and newly delivered to the Soviet Air Force division, Minsk, in 1990, the freighter was seen flying a mission for the Belorussian Air Force to East Germany during spring 1993, already wearing the depicted Trans Avia Export livery. Since then the fleet's freighters have become a regular sight in Western Europe, hauling cigarettes to Minsk or temporarily carrying textiles between Belgium and Tunisia, as well as taking up many other charter assignments.

AVIATRANS CARGO AIRLINES

Splitting from Aeroflot, Aviatrans Cargo Airlines was founded in 1992 at Moscow–Zhukovsky. It was not until late 1993 that their Ilyushin 76T and TDs extended their domestic cargo charters to Western Europe, paying initial visits to the Netherlands and Germany. As an independent carrier, Aviatrans entered a close co-operation agreement with Lufthansa Cargo in 1994, which established its Eastern European cargo hub at Moscow–Sheremetyevo I. The steadily rising exports of the CIS states and an increased import demand for Western goods, resulted in a twice-weekly B-747-230F full freighter service from Frankfurt to the Russian capital city in 1995. The fleet comprises fifteen Antonov 12, 26 and 36 turboprops, and six long-range Ilyushin 76 jet freighters. The flexible fleet, with payload capacities ranging from five to forty tons for single pieces or twenty-foot containers, could be economically matched for onward missions to fifty-five destinations, covering most of the vast territory of the Russian Federation.

Accelerating its full volume-limited load of Belgian-produced L&M Phillip Morris cigarettes out of Ostend, this Ilyushin Il-76T, RA-76754, was about to deliver another consignment on behalf of the Lygett & Myers Tobacco Company of Durham, North Carolina, USA, to be smoked in Moscow during summer 1994. Manufactured for the Soviet Air Force as a military Il-76M version in summer 1979, the aircraft was spotted at Baghdad in late 1982 flying for the Iraqi Air Force in a grey and white livery as YI-AKU. Returning to the USSR during 1987 for a conversion into a Il-76T long-range version, additional fuel tanks in the outer wings boosted the long-haul capacity by twenty per cent, extending the operating radius by 1,700 km. Refitted with civil navigation systems for services with Aeroflot, the aircraft received Aviatrans titles and logo at the end of April 1994, mainly distributing Lufthansa cargo shipments throughout Russia as far as eastern Siberia.

AZERBAIJAN AIRLINES –
AZAL AVIA (AZERBAIJAN HAVA YOLLARI-AHY)

The national airline, founded in 1991, was based in the capital of Baku, operating a traditional fleet of Russian-built aircraft. The first western-manufactured jets were leased in early 1993, when a couple of Boeing 727-235s operated to Dubai, and via Istanbul to London–Gatwick, to Cologne and later to Frankfurt, as well as to Ankara and Athens. Cargo services were initially flown by Ilyushin 76 freighters, occasionally leased from the government or from Turkmenistan Airlines. Despite the self-sufficient production of kerosene, the Ilyushin's higher fuel burn of forty per cent over the B-707 was taken into account, and it was decided to lease a 341C model from the Texas-based Buffalo Airways in June 1994, while two others followed in early 1995. To keep up its fleet of three after a crash involving the company's B-707-323C, 4K-401, at Baku in November 1995, Azerbaijan Airlines purchased another well-used B-707-321C, s/n 19372, which finally found its new operator after months of inaction with Alpine Air at Southend, UK. A threefold growth of oil exports is expected to be reached by the year 2004, since the exploitation of three vital oilfields was granted to eleven oil companies during 1994.

Azerbaijan Airlines Boeing 707-399C departed Baku at the Caspian Sea on an early September morning in 1995. 4K-AZ4 had crossed the Black Sea and the entire European continent to terminate its non-stop cargo flight of 4,000 km at Ostend, Belgium. As one of an initial three leased Buffalo Airways B-707-300Cs, the pictured aircraft had its previous registration 4K-A01 from spring 1995, changed into 4K-AZ4 during summer the same year. The freighters' network stretched from south-east Asia and China throughout the CIS countries via the Gulf to Western Europe, exporting textiles and hauling back supplies for their expanding oil and gas industry, as well as for the field of mechanical engineering. 4K-AZ4 entered services with Caledonian Airways as G-AVKA in 1967, flew for TAP as CS-TBH from 1973 and was sold to the US ten years later.

BALKAN BULGARIAN AIRLINES

TABSO-Bulgarian Air Transport was a joint Soviet/Bulgarian company flying since 1948, but in 1954 the Russian stake was withdrawn and the fully government-owned state carrier developed an international network throughout Eastern and Western Europe. Turboprop aircraft appeared in 1962 when the first of several Ilyushin 18s was acquired, followed by fifty-two-seated An-24s in 1966, displaying the Balkan Bulgarian Airlines titles for the first time. 1968 saw the arrival the first Tupolev 134 jet, as well as of the Antonov 12 freighter. The larger Tupolev 154 medium-range trijet became the flagship on intercontinental routes out of Sofia in 1972, while the twenty-seven-seated Yakovlev 40s were assigned to various regional tasks such as VIP, ambulance and photo survey missions, for which also a number of Mil Mi-8 helicopters were used. Balkan Bulgarian Airlines became a completely independent carrier and restructured during 1985, serving nine domestic destinations as well as forty-two cities in thirty-six countries. A new, modernised livery was applied on the advanced Tupolev 154M series, of which eight units joined the network. The early 1990s saw the end of a long era of pure Soviet aircraft operations, introducing three Boeing 737-53As and four Airbus Industrie A320-231s until 1992. Two extended-range Boeing 767-27Es became the appropriate means of transport for non-stop schedules to New York–JFK, Toronto, Bangkok, and via Nairobi to Johannesburg in spring 1992. Both aircraft were leased from Air France as part of a close co-operation agreement. Yakovlev Yak-42s and Ilyushin Il-114s were expected to be newly delivered from the line to Balkan's regional network in 1996.

Balkan Bulgarian's Ilyushin 18D, LZ-BEH, departs Ostend Airport in November 1993 as part of a steady stream of Western European cargo charters bound for the capital Sofia. Produced in 1966 with 4250 hp Ivchenko AI-20M turboprop engines, fitted with an additional centre section tank and an auxiliary power unit in the belly, the aircraft was deployed with the Polish Air Force during the same year. As SP-LSI, LOT Polish Airlines made use of the prop on its passenger network in a single-class 105-seated configuration, then in 1975 LZ-BEH was integrated into the Balkan fleet. The Il-18 prototype took to the air in 1957, with about 700 units entering service with Aeroflot on passenger services to remote regions in 1959, and it was sold as a medium-range airliner carrying up to 122 passengers. Only three Il-18s were reportedly fitted with a side-cargo door, two Berline aircraft in 1992/93 and a Romavia prop in 1995. The Balkan freighters can live without this feature by loading bulk transports through the standard passenger entry doors.

LZ-BAE, the oldest of four Balkan Bulgarian Antonov 12 freighters, pulls up from the runway at Ostend Airport during summer 1993, leaving a classical trail of black smoke behind it. Initially delivered to the Soviet Air Force in 1962 as one of an estimated number of 800 standard military cargo and paratroop transports, the freighter entered civil services with Balkan in May 1988. For this purpose the rear gunner's station, which had been fitted with two 23mm cannons, was removed and provision was made for a fourteen-seat, pressurised passenger compartment behind the flight deck. Approximately 1,500 of these Hercules counterparts left four plants between 1958 and 1973, which included the civilian An-12B series. Accommodating a maximum payload of twenty tons, ten tons could be carried over 3,600 km. With a maximum take-off weight of sixty-one tons, slightly lighter than the Lockheed C-130, the 3.5m-wide cargo compartment was wider than that of its American counterpart. Balkan Antonovs increasingly started to appear at European airports during the early 1990s, taking part in short- and medium-ranged cargo charters for humanitarian organisations.

CHINA AIRLINES

China Airlines was founded in late 1959 by members of the national air force ten years after the Republic of China was proclaimed on the island formerly named Formosa, situated adjacent to the mainland shore of the People's Republic of China. During the early 1960s, PBY Catalina flying-boats and war-surplus Douglas DC-3s and Curtiss C-46 Commandos carried out charters and domestic services. Five Boeing 707-300Cs and one all-passenger 351B version operated between 1969 and 1985. B-747 models included four of the special performance SP09s, three 209B all-passenger and one 209B combi, as well as two 209F freighters and one 2R7F. Six Airbus A300B4-220s and later six 622Rs were introduced on international widebody services in the Asia Pacific region during the 1980s. Five Boeing 747-409s and four McDonnell Douglas MD-11s arrived between 1990 and 1993, primarily implemented on the non-stop trans-Pacific routes to the US west coast, and on trans-polar routes via Anchorage to New York–JFK. With the company's transported tonnage per kilometre leaping by twenty-nine per cent between 1993 and 1994, China Airlines lay one position ahead of Air China and Cargolux, ranked fifteenth in the world.

B-1894 Boeing 747-209F approaches Luxembourg's Findel Airport in June 1994. Grand Duchy's Cargolux opened regular full-freight services to Taipei in 1978, when China Airlines had just received a B-747-209B SCD combi, and two years before the first new B-747-209F was delivered. A joint-venture agreement between both airlines was signed in 1982, with CAL serving Luxembourg as the only European all-cargo destination, introducing weekly return flights with intermediate stops at Dubai and Singapore or Bangkok. The frequency was doubled in 1989, and four weekly 'Dynasty' flights during the mid-1990s reflected the dynamic growth of cargo originating in Asia. Simultaneously, Cargolux carried out five weekly flights to Taipei.

CARGO LION

Cargo Lion, with its operating company Translux International Airlines, is an all-cargo airline, owning and operating two DC-8-62FH Stage Three hush-kitted aircraft on worldwide charter services, based in Luxembourg. The company performed its first flight on 1 August 1992, carrying medicines, machinery and general cargo to Ghana and returning with over forty tons of fresh pineapples. Since that date, the company has operated regular flights to Africa, South America, Australia, the CIS, the Middle East and the Far East. The name Cargo Lion was chosen by its founder and president Bertram Pohl, in honour of and with the desire to imitate and improve upon the performance of another great cargo airline – The Flying Tigers. Cargo Lion started its activities with its first aircraft, F-GDJM, acquired from Minerve of France (now called AOM) in July 1992, mainly serving Africa. Within a short period of time the activities shifted to worldwide services. Being the only independent European freight airline operating stage III forty-ton equipment during the mid-1990s, Cargo Lion's main activities lay in long-range operations on behalf of major European flag carriers such as Lufthansa and British Airways. F-GDJM was re-registered into LX-TLA when a second DC-8-62F, LX-TLB, joined Translux International Airlines at the end of March 1995, performing its first revenue flight for Lufthansa on 7 April. The company carried out its own in-house line maintenance at Luxembourg, while major overhauls were contracted to major airline facilities. A third DC-8-62F will be added in 1997.

F-GDJM has landed at Ostend, blurring the runway lights with its hot engine exhausts, arriving from Blantyre, Malawi in December 1992 and flying in perishables for the Christmas season.

The original F-GDJM DC-8-62F, now re-registered LX-TLA, and its new sister ship LX-TLB receiving routine overhauls between worldwide cargo charter assignments at Ostend in September 1995.

CARGOLUX AIRLINES INTERNATIONAL

Starting with a single twenty-seven-ton payload Canadair CL-44D4 Swingtail Freighter out of the Grand Duchy of Luxembourg in May 1970, as an initially modest joint venture between Luxair, Loftleidir Icelandic and the Swedish shipping company Salenia, Cargolux Airlines International successfully participated in the expanding air cargo market from its base at Findel Airport. A Douglas DC-8-61CF was leased in late 1973, followed by a DC-8-63F and a DC-8-55F in 1974. To handle the growing flow of goods passing through Luxembourg, the first stage of a new cargo terminal was inaugurated in 1976, and was able to cater for a fleet of up to four DC-8-63Fs in 1977. With the arrival of the first Boeing 747-2R7F in January 1979, Cargolux commenced regular transatlantic services to the US east coast, and became the first European all-cargo airline to operate a dedicated B-747 freighter. With Luxembourg having developed into something of a secret weapon for freight forwarders in Europe, Lufthansa decided to take a stake of 24.5 per cent in Cargolux during 1987, which by then had achieved a ranking among the world's fifteen largest cargo companies after only eighteen years in the business with up to three dedicated B747 freighters. Two further Jumbos, a fourth B-747-228F and a fifth 747-2D3B combi, arrived in 1991 and were successively leased to worldwide customers. In late 1993, Cargolux became the first airline to operate two Boeing 747-400F all-cargo aircraft, delivering 1,000 miles more range, better fuel economy, lower operating costs, and twenty-one tons more payload capability than the B-747-200F. A new cargo terminal was opened at Luxembourg in early 1996 which doubled the existing warehouse and storage facilities. The Asia-Pacific region is the company's stronghold, bringing forth fifty-three per cent of its revenue with frequent schedules to Singapore, Taipei, Hong Kong, Komatsu (Japan), Kuala Lumpur, Bangkok and Colombo, passing through Dubai or Abu Dhabi on the way to and from the Far East.

Flying as the Cargolux flagship *City of Luxembourg* from 1987 to 1993, LX-ECV Boeing 747-271C is just a few moments away from touching down at its home base in summer 1991. This aircraft was added to the fleet of two convertible freighters in summer 1987, which had all originally served with Transamerica Airlines and were transformed by Boeing into the pure cargo role during 1989. This freighter should not be mixed up with the Cargolux B-747-2R7F operating with the same registration between 1980 and 1985, which was sold to China Airlines and crashed after take-off from Taipei in late 1991 as B-198. As the largest European all-cargo carrier, Cargolux operated four B-747-200Fs during the mid-1990s, of which one was leased out to Atlas Air, while the third B-747-400F arrived at the end of 1995.

26

CARGOSUR

Cargosur was established in 1988 as a wholly owned subsidiary of IBERIA Lineas Aereas de España, operating supplemental all-cargo schedules within Europe to the Canary Islands, Central and South America, and the USA. Initially services out of Madrid–Barajas, carried out since late 1988 with a fleet of four converted DC-8-62Fs, included a daily early morning flight to Las Palmas and Tenerife, supplying the non-self-providing holiday resorts in the Atlantic Ocean with newspapers and general goods. Loaded with fresh fruit and fish, the freighters continued to serve key European cargo destinations on the continent, comprising Paris–Orly, Maastricht in the Netherlands, Hamburg and Frankfurt in Germany and Basle–Mulhouse in Switzerland/France, as well as London–Stansted in the UK. The northbound rotations returned to Madrid, regularly including Barcelona. With EC-ELM and EC-EMS, a couple of DC-8-62Fs were returned to IAL of Miami in 1993/94, while a leased DC-8-71F from GPA has been operated since early 1994. The combi or underfloor capacity of fifteen Iberia B-747-256Bs and DC-10-30s was complemented by the remaining couple of DC-8-62Fs and a third DC-8-71F, which was mainly used for services to Chicago via Montreal to Mexico City, to Bogota and São Paulo. Further schedules included services to New York, and via Miami to Los Angeles, while a B-747-256B combi headed via Moscow to Tokyo three times a week.

Completing its homeward-bound flight to Madrid–Barajas is EC-EMD in August 1990, when four Cargosur Douglas DC-8-62Fs were busily operating Iberia's dedicated, short- to long-range freight schedules. Pictured, EC-EMD has sported the warm Iberia colours since the end of 1995. Having collected a countless number of miles in the air on the trans-polar and trans-Pacific network of Japan Air Lines as passenger airliner JA8035 *Taisetsu* since late 1968, this extreme long-ranger's profile was switched into the all-freighter role in the US twenty years later, in 1988. At the end of the year Cargosur acquired the aircraft, which has been in service for a short while with Detroit's Interstate Airlines as N731PL.

CATHAY PACIFIC

In 1946, Cathay and Australian National Airways commenced commercial cargo flights with a DC-3 called *Betsy*, mainly shipping wool between Australia via Hong Kong to Shanghai and Manila. The fleet grew to five in 1947, prior to Butterfield and Swire, a leading British trading company active in the Far East since 1867, purchasing a majority of shares in this promising enterprise in 1948. Over the decades, the airline now called Cathay Pacific Airways grew strong and, through an uncompromising dedication to quality and outstanding customer service, gained the position of a leading international carrier in the Asia-Pacific region. With only a couple of DC-3s and a DC-4, operations started into the 1950s, followed later in the decade by a DC-6 and a DC-6B, as well as a couple of Lockheed L-188A Electras in 1959. The same year Hong Kong Airways was taken over, allowing the airline from then on to serve the vital northern routes to Japan, on which the first jets, the Convair 880-22Ms were implemented in April 1962. The first B-747-267B passenger aircraft was introduced in July 1979, with a first flight to Europe on the Hong Kong–Dubai–London–Gatwick route in July 1980 which for the first time was served non-stop in 1982. Since 1985, B-747-367s have continued to link the British Crown Colony and London over the nearly 11,900 intervening kilometres. Continuing with annual Jumbo purchases, twenty B-747-467 airliners, including one freighter, were accumulated between 1989 and 1996, with the passenger versions being able to carry an additional ten tons of underfloor cargo. On 1 June 1994, Cathay Pacific was the first Asian carrier to introduce the most sophisticated Boeing, B-747-400F, outperforming all existing cargo aircraft in terms of efficiency, range and payload (122 tons maximum). With a second B-747-400F on order for summer 1997, the all-cargo fleet of six aircraft were ranked twelfth in 1994 among the world's largest cargo airlines. Twenty-five Boeing 747-467s, twenty-one B-777-267s, seventeen Airbus A330-342s and twelve A340-211/313s are planned to form an ultra-modern fleet by 2001, including option deliveries.

Cathay Pacific Cargo's first dedicated Boeing 747-236F freighter, VR-HVY, named *Hong Kong Trader*, is seen arriving at Frankfurt in spring 1988. This particular aircraft was acquired from British Airways in 1982, where it served as their *British Trader*, registered G-KILO, on round-the-world cargo routings. It helped Cathay Pacific to increase its cargo and mail revenue by up to eighteen per cent. Europe-bound flights carried sophisticated electronics, valuable machinery, watches and cameras, but the cargo space on return flights was filled with industrial goods. Four B-747-200Fs and one B-747-467F flew in the cargo network in 1995, linking Hong Kong with Europe via Dubai or Bahrain, with each flying five services a week to Frankfurt and London–Heathrow. Two of the sectors to Britain were extended to Paris–CDG, which was served by a third flight via Bombay. North American cargo services routed via Anchorage to Los Angeles and Vancouver thrice weekly, and to Toronto twice a week. Sydney and Melbourne received their loads on three flights per week.

DHL WORLDWIDE EXPRESS

Pioneers into the global express freight and courier service market, DHL International Ltd was the first US integrator to establish itself in Europe, in 1974, rapidly expanding its activities out of the Brussels hub sorting facility. A start with its own aircraft followed in late 1984, when the turboprops of East Midlands-based subsidiary Elan Air operated an 'Overnight Delivery System' to major points in central Europe. The position as the world leader of the international express air freight market was documented as peaking at forty-four per cent of the global share during 1989. Still lying far ahead of the competition in terms of international shipments during the 1990s, ground was gradually lost to the growing American integrator giants UPS and FedEx. Co-operation agreements with 172 airlines carried urgent shipments to 90,000 destinations, all moved by 37,000 employees via 1,600 branches in 223 countries, a number even larger than the member states of the United Nations. During 1995, the DHL fleet comprised 165 owned aircraft, making the hub at the Greater Cincinnati International Airport the most frequented centre of operations since 1985, 240 flights per night covering the US. Five re-engined Douglas DC-8-73F all freighters were purchased from Air Canada and taken into service between late 1993 and summer 1994. More than fifty freighters were stationed in Europe. Converted B-727s continued to be integrated during the mid-1990s, of which some were already thought to be too small on several routes, and it is planned to substitute these with converted Airbus freighters.

LN-FOL, a Lockheed Electra L-188AF freighter, is about to swarm out of the DHL International hub at Brussels on a Sunday afternoon in August 1994, accompanied by the characteristic sound of its four Allison AN501-D13A turboprop engines. Departing on a north-heading runway the flight was bound for Scandinavia to collect parcel shipments on the European overnight express freight feeder network. Since 1991 and for several years the aircraft flew for the Norwegian-based Electra operator 'Fred Olsen's Flyselskap', sporting the national flag and the symbol of the shipping company of the same name on the fin. Delivered to American Airlines as Flagship Tucson in early 1960 as part of an order comprising thirty-five basic L-188A series, the Electra became the first and only American turboprop-powered airliner on scheduled services, launched together with forty units destined for Eastern Airlines.

OO-DHJ, one of eleven Convair CV 580 turboprops in service with the DHL International Ltd subsidiary European Air Transport, is turning in on runway 02 at Brussels National Airport on a Sunday afternoon service to London–Luton in summer 1995. The aircraft was delivered to SABENA in 1956 as a Pratt & Whitney piston-powered CV 440-12 Metropolitan medium-range airliner accommodating fifty-two passengers.

Arriving at Amsterdam from East Midlands UK in May 1992 is G-APEM, a BAe Vickers Merchantman V 953C operated by Air Bridge and named *Agamemnon*. The former BEA Vanguard 953 depicted above was converted into a freighter prior to the merger with British Airways and was sold to Europe Aero Service of France during 1976. In 1987

G-APEM was the seventh and last Merchantman 953C to enter the Air Bridge fleet and was leased to Elan Air for its DHL parcel operations. The aircraft was withdrawn from use under ownership of Hunting Cargo Airlines in late 1992, cut into five pieces at East Midlands Airport on 12 November 1995, and trucked away.

OO-DHX was one of four former American Airlines Boeing 727-223 passenger jets manufactured in 1976 to become converted into freighters and to enter scheduled European express freight services out of Brussels in late summer 1995. With their delivery, the Belgium-registered fleet, which was operated by the local European Air Transport, had grown to a dozen Stage 3 engined aircraft, comprising six B-727-31C/35Fs and six B-727-223Fs. Factory-new Boeing 727-200Fs have been available from the line since 1981; Federal Express was the first to take delivery of fifteen aircraft, which were among the last of more than 1,800 B-727 models produced between 1963 and 1983.

EUROPEAN AIR TRANSPORT

Founded as a flying school at the end of 1971 with Piper, Mooney and CASA light aircraft types, operations switched to charter and scheduled regional services out of Brussels National Airport at Zaventem during 1976. The transition from a commuter airline to a subsidiary of DHL Worldwide Express, becoming part of the first integrated express freight system on European ground, started with the arrival of the first and well-aged Belgian-certificated Convair 580 (OO-VGH) turboprop at Brussels in August 1987. By September 1988 the fleet had expanded to eleven CV580 freighters which were completely repainted into the DHL livery. From 1990 until summer 1995, twelve converted Boeing 727 series 31F, 35F and 223F full-freighter models were speeding up the European medium-range services. The entire fleet serves as an excellent example of the possibilities of a second service life for former passenger aircraft. Re-engined with stage III hush kits and equipped with side-cargo doors, both the Convairs of the 1950s and the B-727s of the late 1960s can be seen on night flight parcel operations at airports all across the Europe of the 1990s.

OO-VGH, the first and most venerable turboprop Convair CV 580, operated by European Air Transport since summer 1987, has landed at Brussels National Airport in June 1989. Manufactured in 1952 and powered by two Pratt & Whitney piston engines as a Convair 340, this aircraft was Mainliner Chicago N73118 of United Air Lines, being converted into a CV 580 under ownership of Lake Central Airlines in August 1966, becoming a so called Allison-Convair CV 580, re-engined with two AN501-D13 turboprops. Three conversion programmes were available by various engine manufacturers, transforming the CV 240/340 and 440s into more efficient and powerful versions. After service on American and Canadian passenger airline networks, the pictured CV 580 was ferried to Belgium during 1987 to receive the full livery of EAT and to serve the European network of DHL Worldwide Couriers. OO-VGH was withdrawn from use at the Brussels hub in late 1991.

EL AL ISRAEL AIRLINES

Two aircraft, a Douglas DC-4 Skymaster and a Curtiss C-46, formed the initial fleet of the young Israel's state-owned carrier in 1948. El Al has since accumulated a mixed B-747 fleet, introducing the first of four all-passenger B-747-258Bs, 4X-AXA, on the Tel Aviv–London–LHR–New York–JFK route in June 1971. Dedicated B-747 freighter services were commenced in 1975 with the first of two convertible 258C series (4X-AXD, and later 4X-AXF), followed by a converted -124F SCD Freighter (4X-AXZ), and a 258F original and pure cargo jet (4X-AXG) up to 1979. Operations of the freight charter subsidy CAL started in late 1976, making use of El Al B-747 freighters on terms of lease. Further Boeing aircraft were added during the 1980s, with two B-737-258 Advanced in 1982, the year when El Al started to operate under receivership from the government, since when flights on the Jewish Sabbath have been banned. Four B-767-258s, of which two had extended range capabilities, were delivered in 1983; a fifth B-747-258B and the first of seven B-757-258s, including a couple of ER versions, were the last aircraft of this type, joining in 1993. The first of four B-747-458s arrived in spring 1994, operating non-stop services from Tel Aviv to both of New York's intercontinental airports, as well as non-stop to Montreal.

Approaching runway 28L at Heathrow Airport in August 1992 is El Al's sole windowless all-cargo Boeing 747-258F (SCD), 4X-AXG, arriving from Tel Aviv and Amsterdam on a weekly schedule. During Israel's peak agricultural export season, 4X-AXG was bustling to Europe and the US together with four sister ships, two B-747-258C convertibles matched for the cargo role, and two freighters of the 124F (SCD) and 258B (SCD) series. In a tragic incident, 4X-AXG lost both right-hand engines while climbing out of Amsterdam with a maximum payload on 4 October 1992. In the aftermath, a B-747-228F, LX-DCV, was short-time leased from Cargolux as a capacity substitution.

EMERY WORLDWIDE AIRLINES (A CF COMPANY)

The 1989 amalgamation of California-based Consolidated Freightways (CF Inc) and the Emery Air Freight Corporation formed one of the world's leading transport organisations offering a wide range of logistic air–sea–land solutions for the specific demands of more than 100,000 customers out of trade and industry. Contracted by the US Postal Service until the year 2004 to carry overnight express and urgent freight, Emery's future is secure. For this purpose, thirty-one jets were serving thirty-one US cities out of the USPS Eagle hub at Indianapolis International Airport. The aircraft fleet of the mid-1990s comprised a total fleet of eighty-six freighters: four DC-9-15F (RC)s, thirty Boeing 727-100C/Fs, fifteen series 200Fs, operating within the US, with a long-haul complement of thirty-seven Douglas DC-8s comprising a couple of DC-8F-54s, seven DC-8-62Fs, twelve DC-8-63Fs, eight DC-8-73Fs and, since 1994, a further eight DC-8-71Fs carrying out express and cargo charter services to 290 points in North America and 100 airports around the world.

This Emery Worldwide Airlines Douglas DC-8-71F all-freighter is seen departing Brussels–Zaventem in summer 1994. Leased from the GPA Group Ltd, this aircraft began a late career as a freighter, retaining its original United Air Lines registration N8079U of 1968, when it was manufactured as one of their pure passenger Douglas DC-8-61s, being re-engined in 1983 into a DC-8-71. Complying with Stage 3 noise reduction standards, the pictured aircraft was phased into service together with eight more leased, forty-three-ton capacity sister ships during 1994, forming the second largest Douglas fleet of the cargo industry after UPS.

EVERGREEN INTERNATIONAL AIRLINES

Evergreen International Aviation, the most diversified aviation company in the world, was founded in 1960 by the entrepreneur and pioneer Delford M. Smith. The first two branches of the group were the helicopter division and the agricultural enterprise. In more than 100 countries worldwide, over 100 types of helicopters and a complement of fixed-wing aircraft were matched to support missions of government agencies such as the UN, WHO and the US Forest Service, as well as to oil exploration and production companies and thousands of industrial commercial enterprises. In 1975, Evergreen International Airlines was established as a subsidiary of the helicopter division. Four converted Falcon 20D biz-jets started domestic cargo charters, and were followed by two Lockheed L-188CF/AF Electras and a couple of Douglas DC-8s, series 61CF and 63CF, during 1978-79. The 1980s saw an impressive expansion of the fleet to cement its role as a worldwide authorised operating company offering scheduled and chartered cargo and passenger flights. The new decade was opened by two DC-9-32Fs and eleven Boeing 727-100Cs, with the latter aircraft being operated exclusively for UPS. Further B-727 freighters were purchased during the mid-1980s and were contracted by CF-Airfreight and the US Postal Service, or were leased out worldwide. Owned by UPS, six out of eight freshly converted Douglas DC-8-73AF/CFs, which entered between 1982 and 1984, were operated by Evergreen crews. A single long-range DC-8-62AF was acquired in 1988. The first of fourteen used and converted B-747s started to enter in 1978 in their applications as convertible combi-freighters, all-cargo and all-passenger aircraft, enlarging the fleet until peaking in 1990.

Using the Grand Duchy of Luxembourg for an en-route transit fuel stop, Boeing 747-273C, N741EV, touches the 4,000m runway of Findel Airport, arriving from the US to continue for the Middle East in May 1989. Originally delivered to World Airways in 1973, this B-747 was the very first of only eleven convertible series models in service with commercial airlines. Intense use was made of the aircraft's application variant as a full-freight, mixed or all-passenger version, being leased to Air Algerie, VIASA of Venezuela, Malaysian Airline System and the Flying Tiger Line. It also carried out a long-term contract for Air India's intercontinental cargo services from early 1986, when the aircraft reverted to Evergreen, flying in the pictured provisional mixed paint scheme shown above for several months.

Carrying out scheduled cargo services on behalf of Iberia Cargo, Evergreen's B-727-185C, N744EV, was temporarily contracted to shuttle between points on the Spanish mainland and, as shown here, to the Mediterranean island of Palma de Mallorca on daily services in summer 1989. Introducing used convertible B-727-100C series to its US and Canadian continental freight operations since January 1979, a total of eighteen aircraft were acquired throughout the 1980s, fitted with side-cargo doors and partly leased out to South and Central American carriers. Built in 1968 for American Flyers Airline, N744EV brought its eighteen-ton payload capacity to Evergreen in late 1987 and was sold to UPS in 1994. Federal Express and DHL took over several of the fleet's freighters during the late 1980s, while quite a number were stored at Marana, Arizona from 1990.

EVA AIR

Two Boeing 767-3S1s commenced intra-Asian passenger schedules from Taipei to Bangkok, Seoul, Singapore, Kuala Lumpur and Jakarta in summer 1991. Services to Penang, Malaysia, as well as to the first European destination, Vienna, Austria, were subsequently opened, while an extension to London–Heathrow was made after the arrival of the first two Boeing 747-45Es in late 1992. A further five B-747-45Es joined in 1993 and increased the frequencies on the trans-Pacific services to the USA and to Europe. During 1994 and 1995, EVA Air's aircraft deliveries outpaced even the growth of the world's fastest-growing region. Six out of the fleet's ten B-747-400s were operated in combi configurations, while three of the ordered six passenger MD-11s were turned into MD-11F (AF) full-freighters. Newcomer EVA Air had brilliantly used its chance to expand out of a strong home market, naturally facing limited traffic rights as a Taiwanese carrier from the Republic of China. A medium- to long-haul fleet of twenty-five aircraft was established in little more than four years, with a further eight McDonnell-Douglas MD-11s on option during the mid-1990s.

Rolling away from terminal CDG 1 at Paris–Charles de Gaulle in summer 1994 is one of six Boeing 747-45E combifreighters of the Evergreen Group; B-16463 was on its way to return to Taipei's Chiang Kai Shek International Airport, flying this stretch three times a week via Dubai. Powered by four General Electric CF6-80C2B1F engines, the pictured aircraft had flown for only six months as *Wings Of Taiwan* for EVA Air, with at least another twenty-five years and some millions of miles ahead.

FALCON CARGO

Falcon Cargo commenced dedicated freight charter services out of Gothenburg's Saeve Airport during late 1986. The fleet's four Electra turboprops were originally L-188C passenger aircraft delivered to KLM between late 1959 and early 1960. Out of a total of 170 Electras produced, forty-one were converted by Lockheed into freighters or cargo/passenger combis, incorporating a large port-side cargo door and a strengthened cabin floor. The future Falcon Cargo aircraft were included in the switching process and became L-188CF all-cargo versions soon after completing their duty time with the Royal Dutch Airline during the end of the 1960s. Three L-188CFs entered Falcon Cargo in late 1986, while the pictured SE-IZU joined in October 1987, coming directly from Detroit's Interstate Airlines. Since then, its new service profile has changed from hauling automotive parts throughout the North American continent to postal services and ad hoc charters out of Gothenburg to points in Scandinavia and other international destinations.

SE-IZU, parked in a fading evening light at London–Stansted in August 1988, displaying a postilion's horn under the crown of the Kingdom of Sweden, with the wider upper cheatline held in yellow, underlined by a dark blue cheatline. The company's name was changed to Falcon Aviation during 1992, and by May 1993 all four big-bladed turboprops were employed with Hunting Cargo Airlines. Three aircraft received Irish registrations, being based at Dublin, while SE-IZU was transferred onto the aviation register of England as G-FIZU, participating in the intensive express freight contract work for DHL out of its hubs at East Midlands and Brussels.

FEDERAL EXPRESS

Twenty-five out of a total of thirty-three converted, and side-cargo-door-fitted, former executive Dassault-Bréguet Falcon 20s started Federal Express operations out of their bases at Burbank, Long Beach, Los Angeles and San Diego to fifty US cities in 1973. Immediately after the deregulation of the US cargo business in November 1977, eight former United Air Lines Boeing 727-22Cs were acquired during 1978, opening the long line of various B-727 convertible and pure freighter versions, which added up to more than 150 aircraft by the early 1990s, forming the integrator's domestic backbone with operations focused on the Memphis super-hub in Tennessee. With the total fleet comprising more than 380 aircraft and the international network serving over 100 countries, FedEx decided to take a bold step and acquired Flying Tigers in 1989, taking over their nine Boeing 747-100 SCDs and twelve B-747-200Fs SCDs in a grand slam which gave access to lucrative trans-Pacific and South American routes, while six of their DC-8-73CFs and seventeen B 727-23Fs were sold soon after in the early 1990s. During April 1994, the world's first two Airbus A300F4-605Rs freighters were delivered to FedEx, of which twenty-five aircraft are planned to be implemented by 1998 (plus a further twenty-five in sequence). The first of an initial number of twenty converted Airbus A310-203Fs were introduced as further fuel-saving fleet entries since 1996.

N304FE *Alison* was one of the first five McDonnell Douglas DC-10-30F all-freighters to resume US continental and international services in addition to the existing six DC-10-10CFs in 1984. Ten years later, in summer 1994 with thirty-five DC-10 freighters in service, the new FedEx livery was introduced to the first of its 478 aircraft. The pictured aircraft was about to leave Frankfurt in the evening via London–Stansted to New York–Newark.

FINE AIRLINES

With a pure fleet of Douglas DC-8F 50 and 60 series aircraft, Fine Airlines Inc started to offer a frequent network of scheduled all-cargo services to numerous Latin American points out of its Miami headquarters in early 1992. Fitted with Burbank Aeronautical hush kits, a proud armada of eighteen freighters provided scheduled trading links between Miami and Costa Rica, the Dominican Republic, El Salvador, Guatemala, Honduras, Nicaragua, and Panama in Central America, as well as to Colombia, Peru, Venezuela and Brazil in South America. Fine Air freighters, featuring the 'Big Eff' on the fin, were also regularly leased out to Latin American cargo carriers e.g. to Midas Air of Venezuela, as well as to Tampa and ATC Aeronaves Transcolombiana. Fine Air offices at all points of their scheduled services are contributing an efficient and reliable operation to the vital air freight market between South America and the US, with further cargo stations at Houston, New York–JFK, Washington DC, Chicago, Los Angeles, San Francisco, Denver and Seattle.

With its nose turned into the sea breeze, Fine Air's N55FB Douglas DC-8F-55 is ready for a first westbound transatlantic departure to Miami from the European continent at Ostend Airport in May 1992. This unusual charter routing resulted from a temporary contract with Tampa Colombia Aerolineas to carry out their weekly cargo service from Miami to destinations in the UK and Belgium. Fine Air's pictured Douglas Jet Trader, N55FB, with manufacturer's number 45678 was the first freighter chosen by Japan Air Lines to perform their international cargo operations in a mixed passenger/cargo configuration in March 1965. As JA8014 *Asama*, the revolutionary Douglas combi carried a maximum of twenty-six tons on nine cargo pallets on the forward upper deck, together with fifty-four passengers being seated in the aft cabin on trans-Pacific routes from Tokyo to San Francisco. In 1982 the aircraft found its home in the Central American region being operated and leased by several local cargo carriers until entering service with Agro Air International at Miami in 1985 and joining Fine Airlines Inc in 1992.

FLORIDA WEST AIRLINES

Emerging out of the Miami-based Pan Aero International Corp, who started cargo charter operations with one Boeing 707-331C in 1981, the trading name Florida West Airlines was born in spring 1984. Operating domestic cargo schedules as well, international flights to various points in the Caribbean and to the Central and South American continent formed the principal chartered freight network. With eight B-707Cs at its disposal during the early 1990s, several aircraft were leased to airlines like Millon Air, LAN Chile, SAM Colombia and later to Buffalo Airways, or were contracted on worldwide charters on behalf of the US Air Force's Military Airlift Command. In summer 1992, the company experienced a profound setback when Chapter 11 of the US bankruptcy law brought all operations to an end. A compulsory reduction of five of the fleet's aircraft was executed, whereby two B-707Cs were repossessed by the Union Bank, and three freighters were acquired by the Irish lessor Omega Air. One year later, in summer 1993, activities were resumed under a new owner who accumulated four B-707-300Cs during the next couple of years, of which two came from Southern Air Transport, one from Burlington Air Express, and one was released from the Union Bank. Purchasing three B-727-200s and two DC-9-31s in 1994, the company became active in the aircraft lease and sales business.

Arriving at Ostend Airport from its transatlantic departure point in Miami during the Kuwait crisis in February 1991 is N527SJ, freshly integrated into the fleet three months before, still wearing the corporate colours of CF Airfreight. The former Pan American World Airways B-707-321C *Clipper Dreadnought* saw service with Kuwait Airways and South Pacific Island Airways, until being leased by CF Airfreight in 1987 and by Florida West between late 1990 and early 1992. Soon after, lessor Omega Air acquired the pictured and re-registered N770FW, together with the fleet's N760FW, in order to find a customer in Northrop Grumman. Contracted by the US Air Force, both B-707-300Cs were flown to Lake Charles, Louisiana in May 1993 to receive the necessary modifications for the military Joint Surveillance and Target Attack Radar System (J STARS). The final mounting of electronic systems took place in Melbourne, Florida, with the first Boeing E-8C series being transformed from North America's first prestigious intercontinental convertible passenger jetliner of the late 1960s, throughout the 1970s, into a freighter during the late 1980s, eventually taking over its last role as a hawk-eyed airborne surveillance platform, soaring over conflict areas from early 1996.

GERMAN CARGO SERVICES

A liberalisation of the cargo business by the German government in 1977 paved the way for German Cargo Services, a wholly owned Lufthansa subsidiary with its operational base at Frankfurt. With initially two Boeing B-707-330Cs flying in 'Curry colours', advantage was taken of the new regulation making it possible to ship various goods of different consignees on one flight. Adding two further ex-Lufthansa B-707Cs to the fleet in 1979, the company's philosophy was to offer full and split charters, satisfying seasonal peak demand by complementing Lufthansa's existing freight services. A capacity expansion and fleet renewal took place in 1984, substituting the four well-aged 707s with five larger and more efficient McDonnell Douglas DC-8-73CF and AF freighters. Most frequent destinations were Africa, the Gulf States, Asia (especially India) and South America. In 1992, Lufthansa decided to integrate their separately operated four B-747-230Fs and two B-737-230Fs with German Cargo Services, with an additional three side-cargo-door-equipped B-747-230Bs to follow after conversion into SF full freighters. The cargo organisation was regrouped during 1992 into Lufthansa Cargo Airlines, which strategically prepared its position for a global network by alliances, successively repainting the German Cargo Services fleet, except four DC-8-73Fs.

D-ABGE, the first of two Boeing B-737-230F freighters of German Cargo Services is, accelerating for a take-off on Frankfurt's runway 18 in January 1992. To comply with the ICAO Chapter III noise regulations, this aircraft was the world's first 737-200F to be equipped with hush-kits, manufactured by Nordam, USA, which were installed by Lufthansa maintenance technicians at Berlin–Schönefeld in 1992. Both German Cargo aircraft originally started services as Boeing B-737-230QCs, together with four other quick-change series delivered to Lufthansa between late 1969 and early 1971. Utilised on passenger flights during daytime and changed into freighters for nightly cargo or mail services, four of them were sold in 1985, with D-ABGE and D-ABHE being converted into all-cargo aircraft at Hamburg the same year. In May 1990 both aircraft were integrated into the German Cargo fleet for two years to fly under the flag of Lufthansa again in 1992; they were temporarily leased to Air Atlanta, Iceland from 1995. The 737-230F can fly a maximum payload of 15.2 tons over a distance of 926 km, and has a maximum range of 2,222 km with 7.5 loaded tons distributed on seven pallet positions. The huge cargo door of 3.40m width and 2.15m height allows a direct onward connection of intercontinental container deliveries within Europe.

GULF AIR

International services were starting during the early 1970s with up to three BAC 1-11s. In 1973 the BOAC share in the airline was taken over by the governments of Bahrain, Oman, Qatar and the United Arab Emirates, and Gulf Air became the national carrier of its four founder states. The first three of five former BOAC Vickers VC-10s joined the fleet in 1974, remaining in service only until late 1977 when a total of twelve Lockheed L-1011 Tristars had started to take over the long-haul routes. The long-haul fleet was complemented by nine Boeing B-737-2P6s in 1977 while Boeing B-767-3P6ERs began to substitute the TriStars in 1988, with a total of twenty extended-range models in service at the end of 1994 serving most of Gulf Air's fifty-five destinations. After the introduction of the Airbus A320-212 in 1992, a multi-billion-dollar fleet expansion programme added the first four of six ordered Airbus A340-311s to the fleet between 1994 and 1995. The short- and medium-haul fleet was planned to consist of eighteen Airbus A320-212s after the first dozen models were delivered between 1992 and 1994. A leased B-757-23APF package freighter was integrated into DHL's nightly express freight services between the Gulf and Europe from 1994.

Reacting to a twenty-seven per cent increase in cargo tonnage handled between 1993 and 1994, Gulf Air added its first all-cargo aircraft, a Boeing B-757-23APF package freighter, to the fleet. Leased from AWAS Australia from January 1994, the freighter was retaining its VH-AWE registration instead of the other fleet's A40 nationality designator. Operating in co-operation with DHL Worldwide Express, the parcel freighter was shuttling six times a week between the Gulf and Brussels. The shown aircraft can carry more than twenty-two tons of cargo distributed on fifteen main-deck standard pallets and in the underfloor holds over a range of approximately 6,900 km. Parked at Brussels, with its 3.40m by 2.18m cargo door opened, it is seen on the week's single daytime arrival on Sunday in May 1995. DHL colours were painted on in the summer of 1996.

HEAVYLIFT CARGO AIRLINES

Specialising in the affordable transportation of outsized items, TAC Heavylift was formed in October 1978 by the two shareholders Trafalgar House Group and Eurolatin Aviation to offer cheap and fast ad hoc full charter services on a worldwide scale. Five bulky Short SC5 military transports were considered to have the appropriate cargo capacity to match the company's demanding objective. Out of service with the RAF, the giant props had to be thoroughly modified to receive a civil certification issued by the CAA. In March 1980, the first commercial flight took off with G-BEPE out of the carrier's operational base at Stansted Airport. The most remarkable aircraft, adding more oversized cargo volume to the fleet, was the Canadair/Conroy CL-44-0 Skymonster, entering service at the end of 1982. A Canadair CL-

44J was purchased from Aer Turas during 1989 and three Boeing 707-320C freighters – N2215Y, N108BV and N109BV – were leased from Buffalo Airways the same year. 1990 was a year of changes for the fleet: B-707s were phased out during early 1990, except a single, British-registered B707 (G-HEVY) The variety of aircraft types was enlarged with the lease of four Indonesian L-100-30 Hercules freighters, offering their STOL capabilities to the market. After the opening up of the USSR, Heavylift saw their chances and ventured into a joint stock company with Volga Dnepr Airlines of Russia, which kept six of their mighty Antonov 124 Ruslan extra-large capacity freighters, as well as An-12s and Il-76TDs, at their UK partner's disposal.

Displaying its voluminous fuselage out of this angle of view at Amsterdam Airport in March 1995 is G-BEPS, which together with sister ship G-HLFT are the world's last two Short SC 5 Belfast turboprops in service with Heavylift Cargo Airlines. The unique Rolls-Royce Tyne-powered Belfast was the first British aircraft to be purely designed as a freighter. Exclusively manufactured according to the needs of the RAF, a total batch of ten strategic heavy transports entered service around the world, mainly to the nations of the Commonwealth, as military C Mk 1 models between 1966 and 1968. After the disbanding of No.53 Squadron of RAF Transport Command at Brize Norton in September 1976, five Belfasts were withdrawn from use, while five were purchased by TAC Heavylift who asked Marshall Aerospace of Cambridge to carry out modifications on three of these aircraft for civil use. Certification by the CAA was granted in early 1980, since when much use was made of the Heavylift freighter's large dimensioned carrying capacity, allowing payloads of up to 36.5 tons to be transported for worldwide customers of the aviation manufacturing and space industry, as well as from oil, automotive and machine construction companies, shipping their oversized components over long-haul distances. Departing with its maximum take-off weight of 104.3 tons and cruising at 566 km per hour, the Belfast could carry a payload of ten tons up to 6,200 km, while 1,609 km was the limit for a maximum load of 36.5 tons. Only G-HLFT was modified into the heavier Mk 2 version, available since 1985, offering an increased payload of thirty-nine tons and a larger cargo volume of 340 cubic metres.

One of four Lockheed L-100-30 Hercules freighters sub-leased from the national Indonesian oil company Pelita Air Service during the early 1990s, PK-PLR was the one to stay longest with Heavylift, until January 1994. Occasionally used as a 22.7-ton payload freighter, the aircraft's primary task was to be at the ready for the Oil Spill Centre Southampton to respond to tanker disasters in the North Sea, a job which was taken over by a Southern Air Transport Hercules, operated by AirFoyle out of London–Luton.

Parked at its London–Stansted base in August 1992, this modified, oversized Conroy/Canadair CL-44-0 was the world's sole *Skymonster*, which had its maiden flight with this blown-up fuselage in November 1969. The upper roof segment was replaced by a completely pressurised and enlarged freight cabin with an inner height of 3.45m, and a maximum inner diameter of 4.24m, in place of the previous 3.28m of the CL-44D4 version. Late in 1982 the Rolls-Royce Tyne 515/10, 5,730 hp driven freighter became Heavylift's most voluminous freighter with a 368 cubic metre (205 with CL-44D4) cargo capacity, filling up a tiny but vital niche that could not be served by other props or even DC-8F, DC-10F, B-707C or B-747F long-range cargo aircraft. Buffalo Airways of USA acquired the aircraft in late 1993, retaining the Irish registration, and continued to operate this unique Conroy/Canadair on continental and worldwide cargo charters out of its base at Waco, Texas.

HUNTING CARGO AIRLINES

The Hunting Group ran Air Bridge Carriers from 1972 and in 1992 became Hunting Cargo Airlines, flying its predecessor's ad hoc and contract charters. It continued operating the legendary Merchantman and Electra turboprops out of Castle Donington, East Midlands Airport in Great Britain. During 1993 the Hunting Group opened another aviation branch at Dublin, named Hunting Cargo Airlines (Ireland) Ltd, which started operations with four L-188CF Electras, and added four B-727-200Fs to the fleet in 1994/95 replacing the Merchantman fleet, which were gradually running short of Tyne engines. Two B-727-200Fs were operated in the full livery and on behalf of TNT. During 1995, four British-registered L-188CF/PF Electras flew out of their East Midlands base, while the very last BAe (Vickers) Merchantman 953C, G-APEP *Superb*, retired in 1996. Hunting Cargo operations of the mid-1990s linked points in Ireland via Coventry with Brussels, served Aldergrove, Dublin, Shannon, Belfast, Glasgow and Liverpool, departed Luton for Heathrow to Brussels, and from East Midlands to Copenhagen, Gothenburg, Hannover, Nuremberg, Budapest, Paris–CDG and Bergamo north of Milan, carrying out DHL contract services.

Prospering from the regular contract charters carried out for DHL, EI-CHZ was one of four Irish-registered L-188CF Electras from Dublin, in service with the newly formed Hunting Cargo Airlines (Ireland) Ltd from mid-1993. The aircraft stands in a row with nearly the complete fleet of sisterships, including the four G-registered, East Midlands-based turboprops at Brussels in May 1995. EI-CHZ was one of the improved L-188C versions with an increased range capability of 4,630 km. Starting passenger services with KLM in late 1959, a conversion into a pure L-188CF freight version followed in late 1968, serving in the US for Saturn Airways, which merged into Trans International Airlines and was renamed Transamerica Airlines in 1979. After being stored at Marana, Arizona, services continued within Canada with Northwest Territorial Airways in 1983.

ICS INTERCARGO SERVICE

Founded in 1986 by Air Inter and Europe Aero Service, two converted Vickers Vanguard turboprop freighters arrived at the Zone de Fret of Aérogare Paris–Orly during 1987. Regularly contracted on domestic night-time services linking Paris with Montpellier, Toulouse and Bordeaux, the first aircraft, F-GEJE, an original Trans Canada Air Lines and converted V952F Cargoliner, took off on its first commercial flight in February 1987, while F-GEJF, an ex-British European Airways Merchantman V953C conversion, joined service soon after. Both were lost: F-GEJF crashed at Toulouse in late January 1988, and F-GEJE last took off at the Côte d'Azur in February 1989. Two Boeing 737-200QC quick-change convertible aircraft arrived during September 1988 wearing the full Intercargo livery to serve their mother company during the daytime on various passenger charters or schedules, as well as being subject to the regular switching process into mail and parcel freighters at night. Two L-100-30 Hercules were leased from the Swiss Zimex Aviation in 1988. Intercargo Service was renamed into Inter Ciel Service in spring 1990.

Spending a quiet day after a late-night arrival from Toulouse at 02.40 hours in June 1989, F-GFZE of Intercargo Service was pushed into a corner of the cargo area at Paris–Orly. Leased from remote operations specialist Zimex Aviation of Zollikon near Zürich, the formerly HB-ILF-registered L-100-30 Hercules started to fly the comparably dull short-haul sectors within France for ICS between December 1988 and November 1990. Independent from external power sources, and able to operate STOL performances from short fields with a payload of up to 23.4 tons, the Hercules left its undemanding metropolitan surroundings and returned via Switzerland to its initial owner, the South African Safair, to operate cargo charters throughout Africa, reportedly in the Ivory Coast and Angola.

INSTONE AIR SERVICES

The origins of the company date back to the formation of Instone Air Line in England in 1919. The company operated as an independent airline before eventually amalgamating with other operators to become Imperial Airways, the forerunner of BOAC which is now British Airways. In the early 1920s, Instone Air Line carried the first known racehorse to be transported by air. The link between Instone Air Services and the bloodstock industry was therefore forged over seventy years ago. In 1976, the company was re-formed by Giles and Jeremy Instone, two of the grandsons of the original founders. Together with its associated company Instone Air Line, a comprehensive worldwide service for the transport of bloodstock and many different types of horses was provided with a variety of aircraft equipped with Instone horse containers. The company now utilises aircraft ranging from small short-haul freighters operating throughout the European continent out of London–Stansted airport, up to Boeing 727, 707 and 747 combis and freighters with the latter offering capacity for 112 horses. Douglas DC-8 and DC-10 long-range equipment, and even the Soviet Ilyushin Il-76, also contributed to the company's tailormade operations. Chartered propliners were Bristol Britannias, Canadair CL-44s, Lockheed Electras, L-100 Hercules, Douglas DC-6s and Short Belfast SC.5 Mk 1s, and of course the pictured Bristol 170 Mk 31M freighter.

G-BISU, the venerable Bristol 170 Mk 31M freighter, manufactured in 1954, taxies for take-off at Marseille–Marignane in July 1987. The aircraft was specially converted for horse transportation. In 1989 it was sold to Canada, flying there as C-FDFC for Trans Provincial Airlines in British Columbia and was the world's last Bristol 170 Mk 31 freighter in commercial airline service. In 1994 the aircraft returned to the UK when it was bought by a group of British Airways pilots. The Bristol 170 Mk 31 evolved from the Mk I prototype, which first flew on 2 December 1945. Initially designed to a wartime military specification, the production of the first aircraft was too late for the war and it was redesigned as a commercial cargo and passenger transport with a seating capacity of forty-four. Out of a total number of 214 aircraft produced in six different versions, 116 served in the air forces of the Commonwealth – G-BISU was one of twelve Mk 31Ms in service with the Royal New Zealand Air Force. Ninety-one of this model were built between 1950 and 1956, equipped with the more powerful 1,980 hp Bristol Hercules-734 engines. The aircraft could take off with a maximum weight of nearly twenty tons and carry a maximum payload of 4,500 kg over a distance of between 788 and 1,650 km, gently cruising at 266 km per hour.

IRAN AIR

Iran Air was established by a merger of the two private carriers Iranian Airways and Persian Air Service in 1962 using Douglas DC-3, DC-4, DC-6 and DC-7C pistonliners and Vickers Viscount turboprops. Modest jet expansion plans materialised with four B-727-86s being acquired between 1966 and 1968. The Boeing fleet grew more rapidly with B737s, B707s and B747S during the 1970s. With the Islamic revolution in 1979, a new 'Airline of the Islamic Republic of Iran' was formed and leased three Boeing 747-2J9F full-freighters from the new Iranian Air Force. Parts of the fleet, however, stood idle and were leased out during these times, due to mutual rising tensions between the operator's and supplier's nations. Soon after, anti-US reaction led to the purchase of six Airbus A300B2-203s widebodies. During the early 1990s, six Fokker 100s and two Airbus A300B4-600s joined the fleet. A new revised colour scheme, leaving out the classical cheatline, was introduced on some of the fleet's aircraft in 1994, still featuring the Homa bird on the fin.

EP-ICC Boeing 747-2J9F of Iran Air Cargo works hard to lift the heavy weight of machinery, spare parts and perishables it has loaded at Frankfurt for Tehran on a hot summer's day in July 1990. Weekly flights to Amsterdam, Frankfurt and London–Heathrow were the only scheduled cargo operations carried out by the fleet's remaining two full freighters, EP-ICA and EP-ICC, during 1995. These were leased from the new Iranian Air Force in 1980, while the third, EP-ICB, was returned in 1988. Pictured, EP-ICC was one of the four nose-loading series 200 freighters without a side-cargo door. They were delivered from Boeing to the Imperial Iranian Air Force between late 1977 and 1978, only serving a few months under the rule of the Shah.

IRAQI AIRWAYS

As a result of the war with Iran ending in 1988, Iraq's economy became weak and it did not take long before another crisis loomed and shadows were cast over Kuwait in 1990. Three months before Iraqi troops crossed the border into Kuwait in August 1990, Iraqi B-727s regularly linked Baghdad's Saddam International Airport with Europe, the Middle East and North Africa, but under the pressure of constant attacks from Allied forces, and to avoid any damage to its transport fleet, Iraqi Airways moved most of its aircraft out of the country into Iran, Jordan, Tunisia and India. Enforced UN sanctions on Iraq after the invasion of Kuwait prohibited any foreign trade, the sale of its oil and any flight movements within its territories, but allowed for imports of nutritional and civil goods. Helicopters were the first to resume internal flights in May 1991, followed by flights with An-24 transports between Baghdad and Basra in early 1992, under the eyes of the UN Security Council.

Offering a spectacular view to the navigator in his 'bomb-aimer's nose' on approach to Frankfurt–Rhein-Main in December 1989, is YI-ANE, an Ilyushin 76MD, coming straight in from a medium-range 3,200 km flight from Kirkuk, Iraq's third largest city in the northern Kurdish province. Wearing the same civil livery as the company's scheduled passenger aircraft, YI-ANE belongs to a fleet of twenty-eight officially listed pure military M and MD versions, initially delivered to the Iraqi Air Force with or without a gun turret. More than twenty Il-76M/MD freighters were reported to have been flown to safety in India.

JAPAN AIRLINES

JAL's new foundation occurred in October 1953, with the Government holding fifty per cent which was subsequently reduced to 37.5 per cent. A weekly all-cargo service was established to San Francisco by the new DC-7F in 1959. 'Tsuru' the crane was adopted as JAL's official symbol, the Douglas DC-4s and DC-7s were phased out, and two DC-8-55F Jet Traders were introduced, one of which was a combi capable of carring twenty-six tons of freight and fifty-six passengers in a mixed configuration. JAL crews pioneered routes across Russian territory by operating Aeroflot's huge Tupolev Tu-114 turboprop in a joint venture with Moscow, which later became an important intermediate stopover destination on the Siberian route to Europe. A steady flow of annually added Jumbo deliveries resulted in a first milestone during 1981, when the fortieth B-747 for JAL was the company's fourth B-747-246F freighter. Ranking first among IATA carriers in terms of international cargo revenue per ton/kilometres, in these days the B-747-100 and 200 series fleet featured several short-range models, of which the 146B/SR had a record seating capacity of 550 passengers on domestic flights. Also the DC-10-40s, active since 1977, were ordered in a domestic and intercontinental configuration, and JAL became the largest operator outside the USA with twenty aircraft of that type. A new corporate identity was introduced in May 1989, replacing the one which had been in use since 1970, just in time to be applied on JAL's first ten Boeing B-747-400 'Sky Cruisers', delivered in 1990. Japan Airlines operates the world's largest B-747 fleet of eighty-seven aircraft. A flock of 'J-Birds', as JAL dubbed its new McDonnell-Douglas MD-11s, arrived in 1994 with each of the ten ordered aircraft featuring a rare bird, followed by the first of fifteen Boeing 777s in 1996.

As N211JL closes in at Frankfurt–Rhein-Main, another daily trans-polar cargo schedule to Europe is completed by this B-747-246F (SCD), one of JAL's remaining fleet of seven dedicated freighters in 1995. London–Heathrow and Paris–CDG were served as two further European all-cargo destinations with all flights arriving from Tokyo using Anchorage, Alaska as a technical stop. Operating B-747Fs since 1974, JAL reached the pole position among the world's IATA carriers in 1981, ranking first in terms of internationally performed cargo revenue/ton kilometres.

JANES AVIATION

HS 748, G-BEKE, passing by in its neutralised Dan Air London colours, owned by Blackpool-based Janes Aviation, prior to hauling a light load of time-sensitive mail and newspaper shipments from Ostend across the Channel to Coventry in June 1993. Three months later, the early production series 1/105 model, designed by Avro but produced by Hawker Siddeley with line number 13, was taken out of service at Liverpool Airport in October 1993. Thirty-one years ago, the pictured aircraft was part of a batch of a dozen HS 748 turboprops ordered by Aerolineas Argentinas. Powered by two Rolls-Royce Dart 514 engines, the fifty-two-seater short-haul aircraft had a maximum take-off weight of 17.9 tons. With only eighteen of the series 1 models manufactured, far more international airlines were attracted by the aircraft's capability to operate from unprepared runways, selecting the subsequent series 2 models, which were offered in heavier and stronger versions, including the 2C version, which had a large freight door in the aft fuselage. A total of 375 aircraft were sold. After fifteen rugged years on the South American continent, Dan Air London purchased G-BEKE for its thinner routes in May 1977. It entered services with Janes Aviation in 1992. Two Handley Page HPR 7 Heralds, a Britten-Norman BN-2A8 Islander, a BN-2A Mk III Trislander, and the mentioned HS 748 continued to operate regional passenger and cargo charter work until the company was restructured as Emerald Airways during late 1993.

JUST – JAPAN UNIVERSAL SYSTEM TRANSPORT

Founded on 19 December 1990 by Japan Airlines, Nippon Express and Yamato Transport as the first domestic cargo freighter company, Japan Universal Transport System (JUST) took to the air in late 1991 with Boeing 747-221F, N8160. The freighter was purchased by Japan Air Lines in late October 1982 and was operated on the company's worldwide scheduled cargo network. Early in the 1990s, the heavy demand of Japan's domestic industry for air cargo capacity was catered for with JUST's one and only JA8160. Since 1992 the aircraft has operated on a sale-and-lease-back basis and has re-entered international cargo services while being sub-leased to JAL. Retaining its unique whale logo and corporate identity, JUST can be seen on occasional scheduled and non-scheduled flights to Europe as one of JAL's 283 subsidiaries and associated companies.

JA8160 receives ground handling prior to departure from Frankfurt's cargo centre in spring 1995 and is seen taking up pallets from a mobile mechanised platform through the side-cargo door. As the cargo enters the main deck, a completely mechanised conveyor system composed of powered pneumatic drive wheels, guide rails, casters and rollers automatically propels and directs it to its precalculated position in the compartment.

KALITTA AMERICAN INTERNATIONAL AIRWAYS

Making his wife's name part of the trading name, Conrad Kalitta founded Connie Kalitta Services in 1965. The company was based at Detroit's Willow Run Airport with the objective of carrying out lucrative car-part charter contracts from the local automotive industry. Pure cargo jets were introduced by taking over a Douglas DC-6, a DC-8-21F and a DC-8-63F from the local based carrier JetWay in 1984, when Kalitta was granted authorisation to carry out international cargo charters. The fleet comprised a Douglas DC-9-15RC and several Boeing 727-100F and C versions when another well-used Douglas DC-8-50F arrived in 1987. To the DC-8F fleet were added nine series 50F and one 73PF and several DC-8-61F models were introduced during the early 1990s when American International Airways was established for worldwide operations, and Kalitta Flying Service became the trading name of the former Connie Kalitta Services. Kalitta ordered five Lockheed L-1011 TriStar 200s freight conversions, becoming the first freight airline to use the fifty-seven-ton payload version in 1995, with further deliveries following during 1996. Two converted B-747 freighters series 132F and 238F rounded up Kalitta's strategic widebody expansion started in the early 1990s, which together with the DC-8 freighter series formed a fleet of thirty-five long-haul jets for a worldwide presence on the cargo charter market by 1995. An extensive domestic network of scheduled and chartered air freight and road feeder services was focused on the centre of operations at Terre Haute, Indiana, strategically based between Indianapolis and St Louis, 270 km south of Chicago.

After having contacted Frankfurt Arrival under its 'Connie' callsign, Connie Kalitta Services DC-8F-55, N801CK, was cleared to land on Rhein-Main's runway 07R in November 1989. As a pure forty-five-ton freighter from new in 1965, N801CK was the second of nine series 50F sister ships which had been introduced into Kalitta between 1986 and 1989. After thirty years in service in 1995, initially with Seabord World Airlines as N804SW, long-term leases assigned it to VIASA and IAS/British Cargo Airlines, and merged it into the Flying Tiger Line in 1980. Used by Challenge Air and Capitol Airways, the freighter served with MPA Pacific Cargo and later for the Northern Peninsula Fisheries before entering Connie Kalitta's worldwide active Jet Trader fleet in 1987.

KLM ROYAL DUTCH AIRLINES

The world's oldest airline was dubbed KLM, Royal Dutch Airlines, by Holland's legendary Queen Wilhelmina in 1919. The very first scheduled flight took off from Amsterdam to London in 1920, when a de Havilland DH 16 two-seater carried two passengers and a cargo of newspapers. Post-Second World War reconstruction and expansion took place with DC-4s, flying via Prestwick to New York from May 1946 and to Buenos Aires from 1948. Lockheed L-749 Constellations were followed by DC-6s and Convair 240s. Throughout the 1950s, DC-6As, Convair 340/440s, Lockheed L-1049 Super Constellations, DC-7Cs, Vickers Viscounts and Lockheed Electras successively enlarged the fleet. Five Douglas DC-8F55 freighters were active during the 1960s. During 1971, KLM received seven Boeing 747-206Bs, becoming the first European operator of the 200 series. Between 1982 and 1985, ten Airbus A310-203s passenger widebodies collected cargo, originating in European and Middle East capitals, and combined their bellyhold container exchangeability with intercontinental B-747 schedules. KLM has the world's largest combi fleet, with only ten out of twenty-nine B-747s being operated as pure passenger aircraft. With a route network covering 148 cities in eighty-two countries on all continents, KLM was ranked eighth among the world's airlines in terms of flown cargo ton/kms, in 1994, which was one place behind Japan Airlines and just ahead of British Airways.

Named after Dr Albert Plesman, the visionary founder of KLM who headed the company from 1919 until his death in 1953, pictured is PH-BUH, the company's first Boeing 747-206B combi of 1975, since 1985 converted into a stretched-upperdeck version. Quickly converted into the combi role, the aircraft simultaneously accommodates 297 passengers and an average of 41.8 tons of cargo. Four General Electric CF6-50E2s are burning an average of 14,400 litres of fuel per hour, allowing a maximum payload of 66.3 tons across the Atlantic Ocean.

KUWAIT AIRWAYS

In 1954, two Douglas DC-3s started to offer scheduled flights under the name of Kuwait National Airways, renamed Kuwait Airways in 1957. The company's growth was abruptly destroyed when Iraqi troops invaded Kuwait in August 1990. Most of the Airbus fleet and two B-767s were seized and destroyed by the invaders at Kuwait International Airport, or were transferred to Baghdad to partly receive the green Iraqi Airways colours. A couple of months later, Kuwait Airways managed to offer limited services out of the company's operational exile headquarters at Cairo and since then reorganisation has included purchasing three A320-212s, four new A310-308s and five A300-605Rs plus holding options on three further series 605R convertibles. The first of three B-747-469 combis and four A340-313 long-rangers entered service in 1995, while the fleet of four B-747-269 combis is due for replacement. A total of three Boeing 707-320Cs, leased from TMA of Lebanon on a long-term basis since 1992, initially flew dedicated cargo services out of Bahrain, before returning to normal services out of Kuwait City.

Awaiting its take-off clearance from Zürich Tower on a hot summer day in August 1992 is Kuwait Airways B-707-327C, OD-AGY. The Lebanese registration reveals TMA as the owner of the aircraft, which operating with its sister ship OD-AGS, filled the post war demand for a full freighter to participate in the reconstruction of the war-torn nation. A third 707, OD-AGX, served only for one year until late 1993. During 1995, the B-707Cs maintained a regular service to Amsterdam, Frankfurt, Paris–CDG and London–Heathrow in Europe, to Doha, Muscat and Sharjah in the Middle East, and to Bangalore, Calcutta and Delhi in India.

LUFTHANSA

Deutsche Luft Hansa AG commenced domestic scheduled passenger, cargo and airmail services in April 1926, systematically expanding a European and far-reaching intercontinental network to South and North America, the Near, Middle and Far East with a large variety of aircraft, until the beginning of the Second World War in 1939. Re-formed as Luftag in 1953, the name Deutsche Lufthansa AG was adopted in August 1954. In the early 1970s, the forty-ton payload capacity of the B-707-320C was still considered appropriate to the demands of the industry. Therefore, Lufthansa was criticised when it introduced the world's first 100-ton payload B-747-230F freighter on 19 April 1972. Germany's home export market however, appreciated the decreased cargo rates offered on the six weekly return flights to Lufthansa's ever-important destination New York. Between 1976 and 1985 ten B-747-230B (SCD) combis were purchased for combined passenger/cargo transportation on the main deck. Operating a total number of five B-747-230F full-freighters since 1988, Lufthansa has constantly ranked among the biggest cargo airlines, successively converting further combis into freighters. Due to German Cargo's success, Lufthansa decided to merge its 737-230Fs and 747-230Fs into the cargo operations of its subsidiary in 1990. In 1992 the board of directors decided to rename the cargo branch Lufthansa Cargo Airlines GmbH. An expanding global network, growing with new strategic alliance partners, reached 450 cargo destinations during the mid-1990s.

D-ABHE, Boeing B-737-230F *Darmstadt*, a former German Cargo jet, sports a new livery after its reintegration into Lufthansa Cargo Airlines in 1992. After twenty-four active years in service as a quick-change version since 1971, a conversion into an all-cargo configuration followed in 1985. Since autumn 1994, an advanced B-737-3S3F has been introduced on European routes out of Frankfurt and Cologne, replacing D-ABHE which was sold to Air Atlanta in Iceland.

NORTHERN-EAST CARGO AIRLINES

With a long-haul heavy-duty full-freighter fleet of five Ilyushin Il-76 transports, Northern-East Cargo Airlines has its base at the harbour city of Magadan, located by the Sea of Okhotsk, a Siberian outpost at the eastern end of the Russian Federation. Founded in 1992 as a subsidiary of Magadan Airlines, the successor of the regional Aeroflot directorate operating fifteen Tupolev 154s, Northern-East Cargo Airlines threw its Il-76TDs into the international non-scheduled market-place, challenging the established carriers with competitive rates and good service. Besides taking part in the transport of oil-related items from Houston to central Asian destinations, an operational base was established at Manston in England to provide worldwide cargo charter services and a special emergency engine replacement service on call. Several of the company's Antonov 12 turboprops have flown to England and are based there. In 1994, Northern-East was still flying abroad in the classical colours of Aeroflot, which still allowed CIS carriers to carry out flights under their name. Northern-East Cargo Airlines may have to switch to its own corporate livery, but this depends on Russia's Air Transport Department, who will decide upon the names of Russian airlines flying abroad.

A Siberian whirlwind seems to race across the field at Ostend Airport in December 1994 when four Soloviev D-30KP turbofans made their noisy impact as they slowed this Ilyushin Il-76TD, RA-76489, of Magadan-based Northern-East Cargo Airlines. Arriving as flight MGD7073 from its last en-route stop at the Belorussian military base Machulishchy, near Minsk, the pilot skilfully maintained a nose-up attitude while the engine's reverse-thrust was employed. This procedure has to be mastered by Russian pilots for operations to short airstrips and this landing certainly delighted the onlooking western aviation enthusiasts. The 1988-manufactured freighter continued on its flight with a short trip of 100 km across the English Channel to Manston in the UK.

MALAYSIA AIRLINES

Malaysian Airways came into being as the national carrier of the new Federation of Malaysia in 1963. Emerging out of the Malaysia–Singapore Airlines consortium in 1971, Malaysian Airline System started separate operations in October 1972 as the fully government-owned national flag carrier. The early 1990s demonstrated the airline's ambitious decision to participate in the growth of the Asian region, accumulating fifty Boeing 737s, mostly series 400 aircraft, including a couple of B-737-3H6F freighters and nine short-fuselaged 500s. Simultaneously, the fleet's appropriate long-haul complement was established, leasing a further three DC-10-30s, two B-747-219Bs, and adding ten B-747-4H6s to the international network up to the mid-1990s. The MD-11 has played a role since 1994, being traditionally leased from the US carrier World Airways Inc, which had helped with additional DC-10-30 widebody capacity on seasonal pilgrim flights to Saudi Arabia in previous years. An MD-11F (AF) and two MD-11CFs were active members of the MASkargo-Division in 1995, together with a first converted B-747-236F, 9M-MHI, while a further two B-737-3H6s became freighters in 1995. During 1995 the airline made no secret of its strategic plans to shift MAS within twenty-five years into a leading position among the largest national carriers.

Malaysia's only Boeing 747-3H6 combi, 9M-MHK, approaches Zürich–Kloten during summer 1992, arriving as flight MH3 from Vienna to continue via Dubai to Kuala Lumpur. Delivered to MAS in 1986 as their first B-747 combi-freighter, the company's air cargo yields were immediately altered by thirty per cent. In 1987 the blue and red livery was introduced featuring a Malaysian kite on the aircraft's fin.

MERPATI NUSANTARA AIRLINES

This airline was formed in 1962 as the second state-owned carrier beside Garuda Indonesian Airways, to fly scheduled domestic passenger and cargo services. Two Douglas DC-3s were the first to tackle this larger objective. During the 1970s the fleet expanded, initially with British aircraft: the Vickers Viscount 800 series, a couple of HS748-274s and a Vickers Vanguard 952. In a co-operation venture with CASA of Spain, Indonesia's young aerospace company IPTN contributed to the Airtech CN-235 forty-seater regional turboprop airliner project, and commenced to introduce the first of fourteen series 10 models in 1988. In 1995, a fleet of over 100 aircraft was made up of more than fifty per cent regional turboprops of IPTN, Fokker, de Havilland and BAe, while an additional forty-four modern Fokker short-range jets worked hard to ensure the transportation of passengers and cargo to many domestic points in the world's largest archipelago state, with a population closing in on the 200 million mark, living on most of the oil- and gas-rich Republic's 13,600 islands spread over a distance of 4800 km from the Indian to the Pacific Ocean.

Dubbed as 'The International Air Freighter of Indonesia', this B-707-323C freighter had only a brief period with Merpati when it was based at Jakarta-Soekarno-Hatta Airport from summer until autumn 1994. Seen parked at Ostend in spring 1995, the freighter had previously served for over fifteen years as American Airlines Astrojet N8404, and then with Burlington Air Express in the mid-1980s. Shortly before Easter 1995, the B-707's Merpati titles were erased and the aircraft entered service with Azerbaijan Airlines. The aircraft's fate was sealed on 30 November 1995 when arriving at the capital Baku from China, when it passed too low over the airport and hit lighting structures not far from the airfield.

MK AIRLINES

MK Airlines (formerly MK Air Cargo) was formed in March 1990, commencing operations in the USA with a Douglas DC-8F-55 (9G-MKA) purchased from Connie Kalitta. During 1991 the freighter was based in Europe, jointly operated with Cargo d'Or of Accra, Ghana, for cargo services between Africa and Europe. The company's second DC-8, 9G-MKB, leased from AECA Carga of Ecuador and delivered in late 1991, was a series 54F freighter which tragically was lost on approach to Kano in Nigeria. MK Airlines have emerged as a leading European-based operator in the forty-three-ton market. In addition to the 43 ton payload capability on full freight flights, 9G-MKC can be operated in a combi configuration accommodating thirty-nine passengers in an aft compartment, still allowing for eight cargo pallet positions. This combination has proved popular with humanitarian agencies, where aid workers, doctors or nurses can travel to disaster areas together with thirty tons of relief goods. This service also found widespread appreciation with customers from international oil companies, the defence industry, rally and racing car teams, and with bloodstock breeders and horse-racing teams. With the complete fleet fitted with Stage Three hush-kits, operations out of Europe are viable into the next century.

MK's 'Kilo Charley', which first flew for Seabord World Airlines in summer 1964, becomes airborne at Ostend in early 1994. The fleet's single DC-8F-55 combi-freighter joined in early 1993 and added crucial flexibility to the operations of MK Airlines, being able to offer customers the dedicated forty-three-ton, thirteen-pallet freighter role, or three possible combinations of nine seats and twelve pallets, twenty-one seats and eleven pallets or thirty-nine seats and eight pallets.

MARTINAIR HOLLAND

Based at Amsterdam–Schiphol, Martins Air Charter commenced operations with regional multi-purpose ad hoc charter services in May 1958. A significant international expansion occurred in 1964 with the integration of two smaller Dutch airlines, and the backing of the Royal Nedlloyd Group as the largest shareholder with forty-nine per cent, followed by KLM with an initial twenty-five per cent minority stake. Subsequently, KLM transferred some of its Douglas DC-7Cs, as well as a DC-8 32/33. A new corporate livery was introduced on the first convertible Douglas DC-10-30CF trijet in late 1973, proudly presenting its new 'Oranje' livery topped by Martinair Holland titles. As an innovator in the air cargo business Martinair Holland operated PH-MCB, the world's first A310-203C convertible passenger/cargo Airbus with a large side-cargo door. To develop its strategy of an operational cargo corridor concept to and from Europe via the Middle East to the Far East, daily all-cargo services departed Amsterdam linking the key cargo destinations Abu Dhabi, Bahrain, Doha, Muscat, and the sea–air port at Dubai, as well as Bangkok, Hong Kong, Singapore, Sydney, Taipei and Tokyo. For this purpose, two Boeing 747-21A convertible freighters were implemented on routes to the world's high-demand markets in 1987 and 1989. The dedicated cargo operations were complemented by long-haul passenger services to a number of markets in the Caribbean and the Far East, as well as scheduled transatlantic services to points in North America. A fleet of six extended-range B-767-31As was built up during the early 1990s, and a third, pure-cargo B-747-228F became part of the system in late 1991. Active in the short- or long-term aircraft leasing business, many of the fleet's jets flew the world on behalf of major airlines. Martinair initiated the fourth major variant of the McDonnell-Douglas MD-11, operating four CF convertible freighter versions and one pure MD-11F by 1996.

PH-MBT, Martinair Holland's latest of four Douglas DC-10-30CF convertible freighters, departs Amsterdam–Schiphol in May 1994. The aircraft's last flight for Martinair Holland took place in September 1994, when it was sold to the Royal Netherlands Air Force for a conversion into a KC-10A Extender by KLM Engineering & Maintenance as part of the McDonnell Douglas ATCA Advanced Tanker/Cargo Aircraft programme. With additional fuel tanks placed in the lower holds, the main deck level could be used for cargo transport, carrying a maximum payload of 76.8 tons over a distance of 7,000 km. Two Martinair DC-10-30CFs were deployed by the Koninklijke Luchtmacht out of the 334th Squadron at Eindhoven, and during 1995 Martinair leased back PH-MBP as their last DC-10 in service for their worldwide passenger and cargo charters.

ROYAL NEPAL AIRLINES

The kingdom at the foot of the Himalayas is the home of Royal Nepal Airlines, founded by the government in 1958. Since then Douglas DC-3s, Fokker F-27s and Hawker Siddeley HS748s have succeeded each other. In 1972 a converted Boeing B-727-1F8 called *Yeti* opened the era of jet services out of Kathmandu's Tribhuvan Airport, elevation 2,012 m. The B-727 remained the preferred jetliner on routes to India and Thailand for many years, and another 116C series was purchased in 1978, while several more were short-time leased. The domestic network steadily expanded with up to thirty-seven destinations served by a maximum of ten DHC-6 Twin Otters. During the 1980s demand was rising for long-range services to the Far East, south-east Asia and Europe. The choice fell on Boeing's most efficient successor to the B-727, and the first B-757-2F8 was delivered from the line in September 1987 with a B-757 combi following one year later. Since the winter season of 1989/90 direct connections between Nepal and Europe have provided an invaluable link for the 300,000 tourists who discover the natural beauties of the mountainous state every year. A leased Airbus A310-304 took over the European flights in late 1993.

9N-ACB *Gandaki*, the high gross weight B-757-2F8C combi of Royal Nepal Airlines, departs Frankfurt in summer 1990 on its twice-weekly service to Kathmandu via Dubai. When the airline ordered its two B-757s in 1986, it was decided to operate one of the aircraft in a mixed main-deck cargo and passenger configuration, launching the production of the 757 combi, with 9N-ACB being the first model of this type when it was delivered in September 1988. Up to four standard containers, with a nine-ton payload, distributed in a three-container configuration can be carried at the front of the main deck, in a combination with between 123 and 148 passengers seated in the aft cabin. Powered by Rolls-Royce RB211-535E4 turbofans, the B-757 is famed for its short take-off capability, with the pictured high gross weight version requiring less than a 2,000m run, even at its maximum rating of 113.4 tons.

NORTHWEST AIRLINES

Originally named Northwest Airways and flying airmail contracts out of Minneapolis/St Paul, the airline was started in 1926 with passenger services commencing the following year. With the end of the mail contracts in 1934, the company's name had to be changed and it became Northwest Airlines. An initial number of thirty-six Douglas DC-3s were introduced in 1939. These were heavily utilised on transport missions to Alaska on behalf of the US Army during World War II. Five Douglas DC-8-32s were operated from 1960, but were sold to National Airlines and UTA of France in 1964. More than forty Boeing 707 jets were introduced during the early 1960s, with a batch of Boeing 720-051Bs arriving in 1961, followed by B-707-351Bs in 1963, some of which had side-cargo doors for combi service. Ten B-747-151s offered the first trans-Pacific widebody service and were complemented by twenty-one McDonnell-Douglas DC-10-40s between 1972 and 1974. A further twelve new B-747-251Bs and five 251F pure freighters were added at the end of the decade. The 1986 merger with Minneapolis/St Paul-based Republic Airlines boosted the fleet by a further 170, mainly Douglas DC-9 series 10, 30 and 50 aircraft, as well as MD-82s, B-727-200s and Convair 580s. Substantial deliveries of fifty Airbus Industrie A320-211s between summer 1989 and mid-1993 boosted the continental fleet to 353 aircraft. As a launching customer of the Boeing 747-400 series in 1989, 16 aircraft will be in service at the end of the century.

N618US, one of eight Northwest B-747-251F all-cargo freighters, arrives at Frankfurt in January 1991, when the Kuwait crisis required every available aircraft to haul supplies from the US to Saudi Arabia. The first three all-cargo 747-251F freighters were delivered in 1975, followed by a further five up to 1987.

PIA – PAKISTAN INTERNATIONAL AIRLINES

Founded in 1954, Pakistan International Airlines started scheduled flight operations between Dacca and Karachi with a Lockheed L-1049C Super Constellation. Early passenger jet services were offered with leased Pan American Boeing 707-321Cs from late 1960, when a growing fleet of thirteen Fokker F-27 Friendships assured connections to more than thirty domestic points. The first Boeing 720-040B arrived in late 1961, and started to link Karachi with London, Frankfurt, Geneva and Tehran, while two more followed in 1962 adding destinations in China. Four Hawker Siddeley Trident 1Es were acquired to enlarge the medium-range fleet between 1966 and 1967 while simultaneously, the intercontinental aircraft fleet grew with seven brand-new Boeing 707-340Cs and four ex-World Airways B-707-373Cs. 1974 saw the next milestone in the airline's development, when three new McDonnell Douglas DC-10-30s and four ex-Western Airlines B-720-047Bs offered increased capacity to the scheduled passenger and cargo network. Widebody services on domestic and medium-range schedules to the Middle East and key Asian destinations were introduced with the first four of a total of ten Airbus A300B4-203s in 1980. The 1980s were mainly Boeing-oriented, with six B-737-340s joining in 1985 and 1986, while PIA concluded a deal with CP Air to receive four of their B-747-217Bs in exchange for four DC-10-30s. Six of the long-range Airbus A310-308s and the seventh B-737-340 entered the network during the early 1990s, serving about twenty points on the domestic market and thirty international destinations. The company's freight work was handled by the two B-747-240B combis, which in a special passenger/cargo configuration had about the same capacity as a B-707C and a DC-8-50F each, or as a DC-10 and L-1011 TriStar together.

AP-AWU, one of four Boeing 707 freighters in service with Pakistan Cargo during the early 1990s, seen here climbing out of Frankfurt in March 1992. This Boeing 707-373C, serial no. 18991, belonged to a batch of four ex-World Airways aircraft which were purchased by PIA in 1970/71. During the late 1980s, AP-AWU was operated in a two-class seating configuration for 150 passengers, until it commenced regular cargo services, receiving the shown new livery in late 1990. Together with AP-AXG, AP-AWU was withdrawn from use at Karachi in December 1993.

POLET AVIAKOMPANIA (POLET AIRCOMPANY)

Seen in Ostend in its new livery during January 1996 was Polet Aviacompany from Central Russian Voronezh, a production and economy region on the Don river, 450 km south of Moscow. The airline started to operate a number of former Aeroflot Antonov An-12/24/26/74 and Yak-40 short- to medium-range props and jets on domestic routes during the early 1990s. A single An-124-100 Ruslan freighter was introduced for international charters in 1994. During 1995, Moscow's airports were the home of most of the civil An-124-100 operators, including Aeroflot (2), Polet Aircompany (1), Trans-Charter (1) and Rossiya-Government Air Services (2). In total, twenty modified civil Ruslan aircraft were active worldwide during 1995.

PRINCESS AIR

This small company's distinctly coloured first aircraft was a British Aerospace BAe 146-200, G-BRXT, which was leased from the Canadian commuter Air Nova. It started its first service between southern England and the Mediterranean in early April 1990. With the arrival of G-PRIN three months later in June 1990, G-BRXT was replaced by the first BAe 146-200QC to be placed on the European market. Flagship G-PRIN, *Princess Alison*, proved its multi-role capabilities in day and night-time shifts. Flying a maximum of ninety-four passengers in a six-abreast seating configuration to medium-range destinations like Venice, Alicante, Malaga, Palma de Mallorca, Faro and on short sectors to Jersey during the convenient travel times of the day, the aircraft was quickly switched into a freighter for nightly cargo shipments to European express freight hubs. The conversion could be achieved within thirty minutes. The BAe 146-200QC could carry slightly more than ten tons packed on to six 108in x 88in or four 125in x 96in pallets, which is half a pallet less than its famous all-cargo predecessor the BAe 146-200QT Quiet Trader, heavily in use with TNT's parcel freighter fleet throughout Europe. The QC series incorporated all features of the non-convertible QT full freighter, such as a strengthened cargo floor and a port-side cargo door in the rear fuselage. Operating with advanced and versatile equipment on a niche tourist market on secondary departure points out of the Greater London area, Princess Air's history unfortunately drew to an early close: it ceased activities at the end of February 1991 after less than a year in existence.

Prior to a homebound passenger charter flight to Southend, Princess Air's own and sole BAe 146-200QC, G-PRIN, *Princess Alison,* slowly rolls through the afternoon heat at Malaga Airport in August 1990. With a maximum range of 2,095 km, the main destination of the Costa del Sol lay within the aircraft's safe non-stop capabilities. Some 108 of the stretched BAe 146-200 series were manufactured between 1982 and 1993, while the aircraft's production continued under the new designation of Avroliner RJ85 Regional Jet of Avro International Aerospace.

SABENA BELGIAN WORLD AIRLINES

With the admission of Société Belge d'Exploitation de la Navigation Aérienne on to the register of companies at Brussels in May 1923, SABENA Belgian World Airways is now one of the oldest airlines in Europe. Initially hauling newspapers and mail from Britain across the Channel to Ostend and Brussels, first regular freight operations were opened between Rotterdam and Brussels to Strasbourg in 1924. With the war reaching Belgium in 1940, the trunk route to Africa had to be operated out of London via Lisbon, while a large number of Douglas DC-3s was acquired, adding up to forty-nine units in the post-war era. The fleet's first Douglas DC-4, *Ville de Bruxelles*, was delivered in 1946, opening transatlantic services to New York in 1947, when the first props of a large fleet of DC-6A and Bs were introduced. Many of both types were subsequently transferred to SABENA Congo where they worked within a network spanning up to thirty-nine destinations. The first eight of ten Caravelle 6Ns opened intra-European jet services in 1961. Fourteen B-707-329s, half of which were convertibles, as well as B-727-29Cs fed the cargo network of the 1960s. A couple of B-747-129s flagships opened transatlantic and African services in early 1971. Delivered between 1973 and 1974, three McDonnell Douglas DC-10-30CFs added their combi passenger/cargo capacity to routes via the Gulf and India to southeast Asia, via Anchorage to Japan, to Africa and North America. The network received a first B-747-329 combi in 1986 and a third A310 in 1987. Early in the 1990s, SABENA's strategy was to develop the European and African networks, which spurred a major restructuring of the continental fleet. Fifteen Boeing 737s of the series 329, 429 and 529, together with Embraer 120ER Brasilias, BAe 146-200s, de Havilland DHC-8-311s and Fokker F-28 Fellowships, as well as three BAC 1-11-500 series, serving sixty destinations on a same-day basis, further strengthened Brussels' status as a European hub. In 1990, a second B-747-329 combi was purchased, followed by an ex-Air France B-747-228B combi.

OO-SLA, SABENA's first of a total of five McDonnell Douglas DC-10-30CF convertible passenger/combi or fullfreighters approaches runway 02 at Brussels–Zaventem.during May 1992, completing its weekly East African round trip to Kigali/Rwanda and Bujumbura/Burundi. Delivered in 1973, OO-SLA introduced the company's new corporate identity, celebrating its fiftieth anniversary. Three DC-10-30CFs left the fleet in 1992 for FedEx, while OO-SLA and sistership OO-SLB stayed until late 1994, with the pictured trijet bearing the colours of the Ugandan all-carrier DAS Air Cargo as 5X-JOE since summer 1995.

SAHA AIRLINES

Saha Airlines was established in 1990, the year after the death of Ayatollah Khomeini, when Iran experienced an increased trade deficit with higher imports under Prime Minister Rafsanjani. A fast-growing fleet was formed with the acquisition of aircraft from the Iranian Air Force. The side-cargo-door-equipped Fokker F-27-600s and Fairchild Hiller FH227s operated the regional transport network, and two Boeing 747 freighters and four Boeing 707-3J9Cs were leased or bought during early 1991 in order to complete long-haul shipments to and from Tehran. Later in the year two more B-747s were leased from the Iranian Air Force, increasing the available fleet number to two 131F SCD and two 2J9F SCD models. Out of twelve passenger B-747-100s, of which nine were originally delivered to TWA and three to Continental Airlines, ten were converted into special freighters at Boeing's Wichita plant in Kansas and from there sold to the Persian monarchy in 1975 for service in the Imperial Iranian Air Force as transports or flight-refuelling tankers. Later two pairs of each model were returned in exchange for four new B-747-2J9F freighters with nose-door loading capability, which were delivered between late 1977 and late 1978. In 1979, Khomeini's revolution changed the country into an Islamic Republic, which fell into war for eight years from 1980 with neighbouring Iraq. During the 1980s, B-747s of the Iranian Air Force appeared for only a small number of flights in Europe, where they were seen at Amsterdam for maintenance and cargo shipments or as aircraft of Saha Airlines in Munich, wearing both a civil and a military registration during the early 1990s.

Saha Airlines Boeing 747-131F, EP-SHC, was spied through an open hatch of a cargo plane at Tehran Mehrabad International in 1993. Besides its conversion into side-cargo door freighter by Boeing, this former TWA Boeing 747-131 model, N93113, received modifications to allow it to be inflight refuelled by KC-135s. The protruding fitting for the fuel-boom can be clearly seen between the flight-deck and the nose of the aircraft. Visible in the foreground is the emergency cable, which is strung across the threshold of runway 11L. Aircraft landing on the 4,000m runway at 1,200m altitude can gain a final deceleration here if need be, before sliding up another few hundred metres on a banked-strip.

SOUTHERN AIR TRANSPORT

The airline's headquarters and maintenance facilities have been located at Miami International Airport since 1947. Southern Air Transport started domestic all-cargo services with a leased medium-range Curtiss C-46 Commando before operating international cargo flights between Japan, the Philippines and Taiwan with two Douglas DC-6As. The first two of an initial three Lockheed L-100-20 Hercules aircraft arrived in late 1969, to be operated on behalf of the US Central Intelligence Agency. A new investor purchased Southern Air in 1973, introducing two further Hercules. The fleet significantly expanded during the mid-1980s, when up to four B-707-300Cs and more than fifteen L-100s, L-100-20s and 30s were operated on US domestic cargo schedules. As the world's largest operator of commercial L-100 Hercules transports, Southern Air became specialised in transporting heavy cargo to remote areas where normal surface and air transportation is not available. (During 1994, Africa was generating nearly half of the fourteen-strong Hercules fleet's total revenues, operating for the UN in Somalia and out of Nairobi, and for the International Committee of the Red Cross in Angola, Rwanda and Mozambique.) The 1990s saw the introduction of five Douglas DC-8-70Fs to complement the Hercules fleet. Fully-fledged entry into the widebody cargo market became a reality in July 1994 when the first of three Boeing 747-200 freighters (N470EV, B-747-273C) joined the 'flower run' in a long-term contract on behalf of the largest importer of fresh flowers from Colombia to the USA, Aero Floral, performing daily round-trip flights between Miami and Bogota. In spring 1995, Southern Air announced the decision to move its Miami headquarters to Rickenbacker International Airport, Ohio, from where eighty per cent of the North American population can be reached within a radius of 800 km, while four more B-747-200Fs are planned to be taken into service in 1997.

N872SJ, the third of three Southern Air McDonnell Douglas DC-8-71Fs leased from the GPA Group since March 1991, approaches Frankfurt's 07L runway in May 1994. The pictured aircraft is capable of carrying a maximum payload of forty-five tons. During the mid-1990s, the Southern Air fleet comprised two DC-8-71Fs and three 73F versions, which were regularly seen passing through Europe chartered on multi-year contracts by Air India Cargo, and by British Airways in summer 1994.

SAUDIA – SAUDI ARABIAN AIRLINES

During the 1950s, and with the technical and managerial support of Trans World Airlines, a fleet of five Bristol 170 freighters, five Douglas DC-4s (C-54s) and ten Convair 340s laid the solid foundation of an airline striving to become the largest carrier of the Middle East. In late 1961 Boeing placed two B-720-68Bs with Saudi Arabian Airlines, which were used to fly to neighbouring states and to points in India and North Africa. Three Douglas DC-6 all-freighters were acquired in 1964, and three Douglas DC-9-15s joined the domestic services in 1967. In 1972 the company was renamed Saudia and two B-737-268C combis were the first of a further seventeen full-passenger models serving more than twenty domestic airports. Seven Boeing 707-368Cs and 373Cs followed between 1973 and 1977, at a time when the decision in favour of a strategic quantum leap in terms of transport capacity was due to be made. The choice fell on the Rolls-Royce-powered Lockheed L-1011 TriStar 200, of which seventeen were selected as the international mainstay of the fleet in 1975. DC-8-63F cargo services to six European destinations were resumed in 1977. Eight Boeing 747-168Bs and two B-747SP-68s were delivered in 1981/82, while eleven Airbus A300-620s further boosted Saudia's growth in 1983/84. Ten B747-386s were added between 1985/86. Celebrating its fiftieth anniversary in 1995, Saudia has grown to a fleet of 106 aircraft serving a worldwide network of fifty-two international destinations. A new corporate identity was unveiled in the summer of '96, changing the name to Saudi Arabian, with a further 61 new aircraft on order from Boeing and McDonnell Douglas, including four MD-11F freighters.

Approaching Saudia's centre of European cargo operations at Brussels in June 1988 was HL7451, a B-747-2B5F freighter leased from Korean Air. HZ-AIU, the first Saudi-certificated B-747-286F, took over dedicated cargo hauling and was joined by two wet-leased B-747 freighters from Evergreen International Airways in 1992 and 1993 respectively, continuing to extend the Brussels services to New York JFK, three times a week.

SAYAKHAT

Based at Almaty, the former Alma-Ata, Sayakhat was founded in 1989 as the successor to the Aeroflot Kazakhstan Directorate, two years prior to proclaiming itself an independent CIS republic in 1991. Situated in the northernmost part of the central Asian nations, Kazakhstan contains the world's largest resources of iron ore, nickel and phosphate, as well as remarkable deposits of copper, zinc, bauxite, gold, silver and diamonds – and, of course, oil and gas. The Space Centre at Bajkonur demonstrates the country's sophisticated technical expertise, retaining strong economic ties with Russia. Trading activities were not only intensified with their mighty neighbour China, but were increasingly resumed with Western Europe and the Gulf region. An all-freighter fleet of six newly delivered Ilyushin 76TDs were in use during 1995, operating out of Almaty Airport at 675m elevation, with the 4,951m high Pik Talgar towering above as part of a wide mountain ridge. In early 1994, a Boeing 747SP-31 of Kazakhstan Airlines made heads turn at Frankfurt Airport, arriving on weekly non-stop services from Almaty. Sayakhat is a dedicated freight charter airline and received six factory-new Ilyushin 76TDs, all of which were of the heavier long-range version with a total weight of 190 tons, directly delivered from Uzbekistan's Tashkent production plant between 1990 and 1993.

UN-76442, one of six Sayakhat Ilyushin 76TDs has touched down at Ostend in October 1993, completing a 3,400 km non-stop flight from Uralsk, Kazakhstan's most western airfield. Manufactured in 1992, the new freighter received this distinctive livery and blue flag with the golden sun and eagle in summer 1993, the national symbol for a population of 7 million Kazakhs, in a country with 17 million inhabitants of mixed ethnic groups. A close look under the fin reveals the wake turbulences generated by both wingtips, made visible by the humid autumn air.

SINGAPORE AIRLINES

SIA had its origins in Malayan Airways which started operations in 1947. The name changed twice, into Malaysian Airways in 1963, and into Malaysia–Singapore Airlines (MSA) in 1966. When it ceased operations in 1971, the two airlines deriving from MSA were Malaysian Airline System and Singapore Airlines, who took over five short-haul B-737-112s and the B-707-300B/Cs of the former consortium. Two B-747-212B deliveries in 1973 initiated the steady and dynamic growth of one of the world's largest B-747 fleets, which received its first substantial boost at the end of the 1970s taking the last thirteen of an order of twenty B-747-200 series into service within three years. A fleet modernisation programme in 1980 introduced seventeen B-727-212s, eight Airbus A300B4s, and six Douglas DC-10-30s, which, including the Boeing 747-212Bs, played an active role until 1985. Keeping the average age of the fleet young, new B-757-212s, Airbus A310-222s and 324s replaced their predecessors during the mid-1980s at a time when most of the twenty new Big Top B-747-312s demonstrated their sophisticated performance on frequent routes to Europe, North America, Asia, Africa and the Middle East. The last three fleet entries of the B-747-300 series in 1986/87 were combi versions, allowing a palletised payload of forty-four tons to be transported up to 11,500 km with 305 passengers on board. The first B-747-212F dedicated freighter arrived in 1988, establishing scheduled cargo services to Europe and to points in Australasia. 1989 was the year of another strategic development, the arrival of the first Megatop Boeing 747-400, the first out of orders for a total of fifty passenger aircraft, including options. Operating the world's largest Megatop fleet of thirty-four B-747-400s and four Mega Ark freighters in 1995, SIA's outstanding growth was financed by its cashflow, deriving from airline's continuous profitability since its start in 1972.

Departing Amsterdam–Schiphol on a homebound cargo flight to Singapore in May 1994 is 9V-SQV. Formerly in use with Flying Tigers and FedEx, this Boeing 747-249F (SCD) freighter was the last of four dedicated cargo aircraft of the 200F series, with the latest three being delivered in 1992/93. With the Mega Ark B-747-412Fs outperforming the 200Fs since 1994, two of the elder models were sold to El Al, and the pictured '9V-SQV' was leased out to Korean Air Cargo.

ST LUCIA AIRWAYS

Founded in 1975, the private company's small fleet of BN-2A Islanders and DHC-6 Twin Otters offered general charter services, connecting the volcanic island St Lucia with its neighbours Barbados and Martinique. For international cargo charter work, especially into the USA, a first B-707-323C, J6-SLF, was purchased in 1982, with another following in 1985. A Lockheed L-100-20 Hercules, J6-SLO, was proved to be the right aeroplane for the company's needs and was delivered during mid-1984. In early 1986 the fleet's aircraft livery was changed into a modern light blue colour scheme. St Lucia Airways suspended operations in 1987.

A few months after entering cargo charter services as the single L-100-20 Hercules of St Lucia Airways, J6-SLO climbs out of Frankfurt Airport on a September day in 1984. Originally delivered to Zambia Air Cargoes as one of the first customers of the civil L-382B model in 1966, the commercial Hercules was stretched by 2.54 metres in late 1969 and became an L-382F freighter with a payload capacity of 21.8 tons, slightly inferior to its twice-stretched successor model, the L-382G, or better known as the L-100-30. After its conversion the rugged Hercules had to prove its capabilities in the high north with Alaska International Air, supplying local oil drilling camps. Leaving North America for the Caribbean, the aircraft was finally sold to Tepper Aviation Inc and crashed at Kamina in southern Zaire on a support flight for the Angolan UNITA contra rebels in November 1989.

TAROM – TRANSPORTURILE AERIENE ROMANE

Coming into being as the national, fully government-owned state carrier of Romania in 1954, TAROM expanded its domestic network with Soviet Lisunov Li-2s, manufactured under a licensing agreement with Douglas as a derivative of the DC-3. With the first delivery of a BAe (BAC) One-Eleven in summer 1968, sixteen further series 400 and 525FTs had been introduced to TAROM's European trunk routes out of Bucharest, Timisoara and Constanta by 1981. During the mid-1970s, a fleet development took shape with the introduction of five Ilyushin 62s and four Boeing 707-300Cs on long-haul routes, as well as eleven Tupolev 154s. The short-haul Western type of aircraft secured the carrier's appreciation, and with authorisation from England nine Romanian-manufactured RomBac One-Eleven 560s rolled out between 1982 and 1991, while many of the British BACs were leased out to smaller European, Mediterranean and African operators. The first two of three Airbus Industrie A310-325 (ET)s arrived in late 1992 flying on intercontinental passenger schedules.

While aircraft YR-ABA and -ABC were B-707-3K1Cs delivered from the line in 1974, YR-ABM and the pictured YR-ABN enjoyed preliminary careers with Pan American World Airways until entering services with TAROM in 1975 and 1976 respectively. After years of scheduled passenger services out of Bucharest serving points from the Far East to the USA, the convertible jets followed several worldwide cargo charter assignments on behalf of African and South American carriers. Liveries were changed several times, and the national flag design, as seen on YR-ABN, was painted on in Hamburg during summer 1990.

FLYING TIGERS

Shortly after the Second World War in 1945, National Skyway Freight Corporation (NSFC) was the first US all-cargo airline to start coast-to-coast services out of Burbank, California. It used fourteen clumsy, ex-Navy, Budd RB-1 Conestogas acquired from the War Surplus Board. The first flight crews were Curtiss P-40 veterans of the 1941/42 Flying Tiger Group, so the founder, Robert Prescott, renamed the company the Flying Tiger Line in 1946. In 1947, when the Civil Aeronautics Board granted their approval for scheduled cargo services, a lucrative contract was signed with the USAF Air Transport Command to supply the trans-Pacific bases in Asia with twenty-eight weekly flights, carried out by a fleet of Douglas C-47s and C-54s (DC-3 and DC-4 cargo versions). New automated cargo terminals at Chicago–O'Hare and New York–JFK were inaugurated in 1965 to prepare the company for its role as the leading company in the early days of the expanding air cargo industry. With the arrival of the first of ten Douglas Super DC-8-63Fs in 1968, headquarters were moved from Burbank to Los Angeles International Airport. Receiving the CAB licences for scheduled cargo services from the US to Asia during 1969, the Flying Tiger Line changed its name to Tiger International,

regularly serving the company's hubs at Tokyo, Seoul, Manila, Hong Kong, Kuala Lumpur, Singapore, Saigon and Bangkok. The decision to purchase the 747 freighter was a logical step and in September 1974 the first of six B-747-123SFs arrived from Boeing's Wichita plant, after being converted from the '100' passenger series. In 1978, the Tiger International conglomerate decided to take a 15.6 per cent stake in Seabord World Airlines, founded 1946 in Washington DC, offering cargo services on transatlantic routes since 1955. On 1 October 1980, a $400,000,000 merger of both all-cargo companies created the world's largest air cargo carrier, trading as Flying Tigers. From that date the combined fleet of sixteen Boeing 747-100 and 200 freighters, twenty-one DC-8-63CFs and seven DC-8-61CFs had unlimited access to a worldwide route network. Boeing 727 freighters entered the fleet in 1984, and during 1986 a weekly round-the-world routing was inaugurated. The name of Federal Express rose rapidly over the horizon when it purchased the Flying Tigers for $850,000,000 in January 1989, thus ending a legendary airline that had carried its bright colours across the world since the Second World War.

'Tiger 015 airborne': climbing out of Frankfurt, pictured is N810FT Boeing 747-249F *Clifford C. Groh* in December 1988 during the last months of operation under the Flying Tiger callsign. In October 1979 the first of four 747-249F series joined the 132SF versions, and with the addition of six 747-245Fs containerships from Seabord World Airways in 1980, the world's largest all-cargo fleet had been formed. After services under FedEx as N633FE, the pictured freighter was operated on lease by American International Airways for a few months, to join Air Hong Kong's pure B-747F fleet hired from the Polaris Aircraft Leasing Corporation in March 1994.

TMA OF LEBANON (TRANS MEDITERRANEAN AIRWAYS)

Three years after the opening of the new Beirut International Airport in 1950, Trans Mediterranean Airways (TMA) started to offer non-scheduled cargo charter services with two Avro 685 Yorks. With the completion of two 2,400m runways in 1954, Beirut became an important crossroads for the region and an international transit point for long-haul flights from Europe to Asia and Australia. Transformed into a joint stock company in 1959, TMA was certificated as a scheduled all-cargo carrier initially operating with a couple of Douglas DC-4 pistonliners, but adding further C-54s to the fleet and operating a total of seven Skymasters in 1962. Worldwide jet cargo services were introduced in 1966 with a first Boeing B-707-327C. By 1973, eight further cargo jets had entered the fleet's international route network. In May 1975 a firstly leased and later purchased ex-American B-747-123F, OD-AGC, commenced regular cargo schedules between Beirut, Amsterdam and New York, as well as to London. The second, OD-AGM, followed in June 1976, at a time which unfortunately coincided with the breakout of the civil war, when Beirut Airport had to be closed for more than a year. Selling the 747s in 1977, TMA strived for a fleet development by relying on the indestructible Boeing B-707-320C, adding four more used, converted all-cargo versions within one year after May 1977. Since 1992, three of seven TMA B-707Cs were operated on behalf of Kuwait Airways on long-term charter contracts, with the aircraft wearing full Kuwaiti liveries but retaining their Lebanese registrations. During 1993, OD-AGX returned to TMA and joined the remaining three B-707Cs. TMA's exclusive Stage II certificated freighters were still present in Europe at Amsterdam, Basle, Frankfurt, London LHR and Paris Orly, during the mid-1990s, maintaining more than daily cargo schedules via Bahrain to six destinations in Asia and the Far East as well as throughout the Gulf, while undergoing negotiations with aviation authorities for continued operations proved crucial for TMA's future fleet policy.

Decelerating with extended leading-edge flaps after landing under its 'Tango-Lima' callsign at Ostend in October 1990 is OD-AGY of TMA, Lebanon. This aircraft was leased in 1971 as one of TMA's partial fleet of six former Braniff Airways B-707-327Cs, and was delivered to the Dallas-based carrier in May 1966 as N7096, with its fuselage completely painted yellow. This must have inspired TMA to use a quite similar colour scheme on their own aircraft. Further TMA freighters were acquired from American Airlines, Pan American and Trans World Airlines, as well as from Aer Lingus. Five TMA B-707s have been lost since the 1980s due to bombing and shelling at Beirut, and incidents at Tokyo and Amsterdam.

TNT INTERNATIONAL AVIATION SERVICES

The Windsor-based British subsidiary of TNT Worldwide Express started operations with its first BAe 146-200QT Quiet Trader, G-TNTA, out of Birmingham Airport in May 1987, emerging to build up an extensive intra-European overnight express freight system. After trials with the prototype BAe 146-200QT had revealed the efficiency and environmental adaptability of the latest product of British Aerospace, the TNT Group announced its intention to place options for a total of seventy-two Quiet Traders in December 1986, which already included the larger 300QT series. During mid-1988, the UK Birmingham operations were moved to Luton Airport, north of London. In 1991 TNT Express Worldwide became the new name for the world's largest diversified transport company. It came into being through the merger of TNT Skypak and TNT Express Europe (formerly TNT IPEC). A further step forward was the joint venture between TNT Ltd and GD Net BV (Global Delivery Network), a governmental consortium of five national mail authorities, in 1992. In the mid-1990s, a European network of more than thirty destinations is focused on Cologne during the night, when eleven BAe 146 QT series 200s, nine series 300s, five Boeing 727-200Cs operated by Hunting Cargo Airlines and three Fokker F-27-600s of GD Net exchange their loads and return to their point of departure in the early morning hours. As a result of expansion possibilities at Cologne, TNT has chosen Liège–Bierset Airport, only 150 km to the west in Belgium, for its new operational base from the late 1990s.

No noisy reverse-thrust is necessary to bring AirFoyle's second BAe 146-200QT, G-TNTB, to a halt at its new TNT base at Luton Airport in August 1988. The variable airbrake and the upper wing lift spoilers do a silent job while landing on runway 26. Subsequently converted into the dedicated full-freighter role after its roll-out as a Quiet Trader by Hayes International Corporation (later Pemco Aeroplex) at Dothan, Alabama, USA during 1987, G-TNTB flew its first revenue service for TNT Roadfreight (UK) Ltd on 21 September the same year. Flying into Cologne's night curfew was not a problem with the four Textron Lycoming ALF 502R-5 turbofans, making the BAe 146 series the quietest aircraft available. Loaded with six and a half pre-packed containers of 1,600 kg carrying capacity each, the 200QT could be turned around within twenty minutes.

TURKISH AIRLINES

Following Kemal Atatürk's objective, that the future lies in the skies, Devlet Hava Yollari was established in May 1933 as the State Airlines Administration of Turkey. Renamed in 1957, THY Turkish Airlines introduced five Vickers Viscount 794D turboprops in 1958. Five Fokker F-27-100s helped to expand the international network to central Europe and the Near East from the early 1960s, until the first leased Douglas DC-9-15 took over in 1967. Eight DC-9-32s joined up to 1972, followed by a further two up to 1976. THY was nationalised in 1977, and operated exclusive of all foreign capital. The first dedicated freight services were started with two B-707-321Cs, primarily hauling fruit, vegetables and fish, leather and textiles on scheduled flights from Istanbul to Frankfurt, where onward transatlantic loads to the US were transshipped aboard DC-8Fs and B-747Fs of the Flying Tigers. By 1991, fourteen A310s were deployed on domestic trunk routes, while the extended-range 304 series aircraft linked Turkey internationally. The B-727-2F9 and Airbus A310 fleets were complemented by a medium-range fleet of B-737-400s in 1991, including a couple of series 500 aircraft, which together totalled twenty-eight aircraft during the mid-1990s. The first two of five Airbus A340-311 long-haulers became active on non-stop routes to the US east coast and Japan in 1993, while five Avro RJ70s and ten RJ100 Avroliners played their domestic and international roles.

TC-JCA *Edirne* has just landed at Maastricht–Aachen Airport in October 1995. Manufactured in 1982, it was one of the last six B-727 aircraft produced. New corporate livery was introduced on TC-JCA in late 1989 when it was still operating as a pure 167-seat passenger airliner. With Maastricht being most conveniently situated at the German and Belgian border, the small Dutch airport was chosen by Turkish Airlines to supply its perishables into the heart of central Europe's most populated industrial region.

TURKMENISTAN AIRLINES (TURKMENAVIA)

The former Aeroflot Turkmenistan Directorate became independent as Turkmenavia with the establishment of a Sunnite Muslim republic in 1991. Three divisions were formed: Akhal Aircompany in the capital Ashkhabad, Khazar Aircompany in Krasnovodsk at the Caspian Sea, and Lebap Aircompany in Chardzou. The latter two divisions' fleets mainly comprised Antonov 2 biplane freighters and sprayers, and Antonov 24 and 26 models, as well as Mil Mi-8 helicopters and Yakovlev 40 jets. All three airports were connected by the country's single railway line. Flights were operated under the divisions' own three-letter designators, while the aircraft were bearing the full colour scheme of Turkmenavia. Three Antonov 26 combi versions and four Ilyushin 76TDs formed the cargo fleet of the Akhal company during 1993, while twenty Mil Mi-8 helicopters, thirteen-ton take-off weight utility, were used as freighters as well. A growing fleet of Antonov 24s and a modest number of Yakovlev 40 and 42D passenger aircraft were complemented by twelve Tu-154s, of which one was used as a freighter, and three B-737-300s and a single B-757-23A, which was operated as part of the presidential flight.

EZ-F422 of Turkmenistan's Akhal division caught at a precarious moment on the runway at Ostend. Notice how the main undercarriage is still airborne as the nose-wheels take the strain – a good example of what can happen in the strong cross-winds that frequently occur at this airport situated by the sea. The shown Ilyushin Il-76TD civil long-range version was the second out of a fleet of four, which was delivered direct from Uzbekistan's Tashkent factory in 1992.

UNIFLY EXPRESS

The company started in 1978 by providing executive charters with Cessna turboprops and Citation jets out of Rome's Ciampino Airport. The first larger jets were acquired in October 1986, when two Fokker F-28 1000 Fellowships offered a seating capacity for sixty-five passengers each. During the late 1980s, when both aircraft were leased out to Milan–Linate-based Alinord, a couple of beautiful red Douglas DC-9-15RC convertible freighters became available for cargo charters and express freight shipments throughout Europe in 1988. This was the year of expansion, while four Irish-registered passenger aircraft of the heavier McDonnell-Douglas MD-80 series were leased from the GPA Group and Irish Aerospace. Operating international passenger charters from various Italian airports, several MD-80s were short-time leased to various airlines, while two MD-83s spent a couple of months with the newly established German Wings of Munich. Unifly's three MD-83s and the single MD-82 had to be returned to Ireland in early 1990, and the company also offered their seven-placed MD-80 orders to other carriers. Continuing with international cargo services with their DC-9-15RCs until summer 1991, both aircraft were eventually sold to Fortune Aviation.

A beautiful example of the last aircraft type designed by the Douglas Aircraft Corporation. It was built in the mid-1960s and is known as a 'Rapid Change' Douglas DC-9-15RC with side-cargo door, and is a convertible passenger/cargo version. During summer 1988, I-TIAR was chartered by Alitalia in its all-cargo configuration on up to four flights a week between Rome and Frankfurt. With its sister ship I-TIAN, I-TIAR was one of eighteen series 15RC short-haul airliners delivered to Continental Air Lines in 1967/68. Its career continued on the North American continent, flying with Air Canada, Air Florida, Emerald Airlines and the Purolator Courier Service. The DC-9-15 was a basic DC-9-10 series fitted with stronger JT8D-1 engines, allowing a maximum take-off weight of forty-one tons and a range of 2,500 km.

UPS UNITED PARCEL SERVICE

UPS has a fleet of over 500 aircraft comprising about 200 owned and 300 leased cargo jets. The owned fleet was initially established with B-727 convertibles taken into service during 1982, topped up by fifty-nine trijets of this type in 1995. These were successively re-engined into 727QFs, the first of the Rolls-Royce RB651-54 Tay-powered Quiet Freighters that complied with Stage 3 noise regulations, indispensable on most noise-sensitive European airports during night-time. The UPS all-freighter long-range fleet of 1995 comprised twenty-four DC-8-71Fs and twenty-eight series 73Fs, twelve B-747-100Fs with side-cargo doors, plus three SR46 short-range models. Thirty orders with Boeing for the B-757-24APF in 1987 launched the forty-ton payload Parcel Freighter programme, actually operating fifty aircraft with fifteen on order. The first flight of the B-767-34AF Extended Range UPS freighter took place on 20 June 1995; thirty are on order.

Three former Flying Tiger Douglas DC-8-63Fs were the first to enter the UPS fleet as converted DC-8-73Fs at the end of 1982. The fourth re-engined aircraft was N808UP purchased in 1983, seen here approaching the UPS Europe hub at Cologne/Bonn in October 1995. The world's largest DC-8 fleet of the 1990s gained a massive injection between 1984 and 1986 when thirty-seven series 71F and 73F freighters became the backbone of operations.

UZBEKISTAN AIRWAYS

Uzbekistan Airways is the national carrier of the largest central Asian nation with a population of more than 21 million, of which nearly eighty per cent are Sunnite Muslims. Like its neighbour state Kazakhstan, Uzbekistan took advantage of its rich mineral resources, mainly relying on gas and the produce of cotton. Five Antonov 12 freighters handle the regional transport work, while nineteen civil versions of the Ilyushin 76TD were delivered from the local plant at Tashkent-East between 1989 and 1993, flying in various liveries. With technical assistance from Lufthansa, two former Ecuatoriana Airbus 310-324s were introduced for non-stop passenger services to Frankfurt and London in summer 1993. Due to an overcapacity, Uzbekistan Airways leased out several of its fleet to China, Pakistan and to the United Nations for worldwide operations. International Il-76TD cargo charter services were carried out to serve destinations in Russia, Uzbekistan's largest trading partner, and other CIS members, as well as to points in Asia, the Middle East, especially into the Gulf region, and key European cargo destinations.

Pristine and only a few months old, this Ilyushin 76TD, UK-76359, displays Uzbekistan's national colours in perfect showroom condition on a sunny day in August 1993 at Zürich-Kloten. First seen at Tashkent-East's Ilyushin manufacturing plant in mid-May 1993, the freighter was soon chartered by Air India to operate twice-weekly scheduled cargo services from Delhi to Zürich and back to Bombay. Flying the 4,900 km non-stop between Tashkent and Zürich was only possible by reducing the maximum payload of forty tons; a range of 7,300 km could be achieved with twenty tons loaded. Its large wing, designed for tactical short field operations, induces such a high drag on long-range flights that Sergei V. Ilyushin's masterpiece of curved lines consumes forty per cent more kerosene than a Boeing 707-300C and the Douglas DC-8-50F and 60F series. Evergreen International and Southern Air Transport became the successors on this route using their Douglas DC-8-73Fs between India, Europe and the US during summer 1994.

VOLGA-DNEPR AIRLINES RUSSIAN INTERNATIONAL CARGO AIRLINES

This joint stock company was established in 1990 by its three major shareholders, the Ukrainian Antonov Design Bureau, the engine manufacturer Motor Sich and the Russian Aviastar production plant at Ulyanovsk. Having been detached from the former Aeroflot monolith, it was renamed after the two principal rivers of the region. In September 1991, Ulyanovsk-based Volga-Dnepr Airlines introduced its first An-124 to the fleet and this pioneered a joint venture with Europe's outsize specialist, Heavylift Cargo Airlines from London–Stansted. Six of the 150-ton capacity freighters owned by Volga-Dnepr Airlines in early 1993 operated in co-operation with its British partner.

Using Luxembourg as an intermediate stopover point between Russia and the USA during December 1994 are two Volga-Dnepr Antonov 124-100 Ruslan freighters, running their powerful APUs prior to a regular transatlantic flight to Houston, Texas. The three circles, being part of and edging into the blue wrap-around cheatline of the tail fin, presented the stylised letters ADB, the symbol of the Antonov Design Bureau. The fin projecting in the background belongs to RA-82044, additionally containing Heavylift's white H in a small red field, demonstrating its alliance with that British cargo airline.

ZANTOP INTERNATIONAL AIRLINES

Established by the Zantop family in 1972, the main business of this Detroit-based all-cargo operator had its roots in contracts with the automobile industry, importing deliveries via Willow Run Airport, Michigan. A DC-6BF was the first of ten Douglas piston liners which formed the early fleet, some being leased and later purchased, from the airline's beginnings until 1975. Parallel to that, ten third-hand Convair side-cargo-door turboprop freighters, manufactured in the early 1950s and upgraded into CV640F versions in 1966, arrived in 1973, taking to the skies for general cargo charters throughout the US. Proceeding with its continuous expansion, nineteen Lockheed L-188AF and CF Electras joined the existing turboprop cargo fleet between 1974 and the end of that decade. The first jet freighter, a Douglas DC-8F-54, entered the fleet in late 1978, and was the only addition until seven DC-8-62AF long-range freighters were acquired between 1984 and 1985. With their acquisition, charter and contract services were also carried out on a worldwide scale, until all DC-8-62AFs were sold to CF Airfreight in 1988. The large and ageing fleet of nineteen Lockheed Electras, and ten Convair 640Fs continued to fly extensive domestic charters, while two Electras were leased to Channel Express of the UK; some aircraft were stored at Detroit–Willow Run, while a number of them were based in Alaska, flying regular multi-leg services out of Anchorage. Three Douglas DC-8F-54 Jet Traders were at the ready for the continental and international jet cargo market in 1995.

Seen at Frankfurt in October 1987 is N811ZA, one of seven Douglas Super DC-8-62AF all-freighter series operating with Zantop between 1984 and 1988. Manufactured by Douglas in 1972, N811ZA had line number 554 and was one of the last of a total of 556 DC-8 models built. Japan Air Lines took advantage of the pictured aircraft's efficient service at extreme ranges, implementing the freighter on trans-polar, trans-Pacific and on the trans-Siberia routes out of Tokyo. The DC-8-62 was a redesign of the existing DC-8-10/20/30/40 and 50 series, being stretched by 2.03m and featuring a new wing with an increased span, new full-length engine pod cowlings and an increased fuel capacity. During 1988, all Zantop Super 62s were sold to CF Airfreight and were transferred to Emery Worldwide Airlines during 1991. In the spirit of Douglas, who had created an aircraft to last, McDonnell Douglas continued this tradition and maintained its outstanding product support for the DC-8. A hush kit was certified in the early 1990s, meeting the ICAO Chapter III noise regulations and extending the operational life well into the next decade.

ADC AIRLINES AVIATION DEVELOPMENT COMPANY LTD

Based at Ikeja, at Murtala Mohammed Airport in Lagos, Nigeria, ADC Airlines commenced domestic passenger services with three original Braniff Airways BAe (BAC) One-Eleven short-haul aircraft. The first 203AE series arrived in December 1990, and was followed by another 200 and a 400 series in April 1991, all being leased from the Irish GPA Group. A couple of Douglas DC-9-31s joined in October 1992, extending services to West African capitals on scheduled flights later in the course. The company's profile shifted to worldwide ad hoc cargo charters in spring 1994 when purchasing their sole Boeing 707-338C freighter, 5N-BBD, which was rolled out at Shannon, freshly painted in the striking

blue and red corporate design with the feather symbol. Previously, the company's air cargo operations to Europe were carried out by chartered African Boeing 707-300C aircraft flying under the ADK three-letter designator of ADC Aviation Development Company, regularly routing out of Ostend via London's Gatwick or Heathrow airports to Nigeria and other West African destinations. ADC Airlines maintain their hold on the European forty-ton payload market to Africa during the mid-1990s. Three former TWA Boeing 727-231s of 1969 vintage were ferried from the US to Nigeria in 1995, finding enough work for the rest of their lives, while the last fleet entry was a short-haul regional ATR 42-300 turboprop.

5N-BBD, ADC's sole B-707-338C freighter, has landed at Ostend Airport in March 1995. Originally manufactured for Qantas as VH-EAE *City of Brisbane* in 1968, the aircraft was purchased by ITEL Corporation ten years later in 1978, and was leased to British Midland Airways. Flagged under the Union Jack as G-BFLD until 1985, the BMA jet was sub-leased on short terms to Kuwait Airways, Air Algerie and DETA Mozambique

Airlines, and became a common sight in US airspace during the mid-1980s. On lease to Burlington Air Express as N862BX, operations were carried out by crews of Southern Air Transport until the freighter was temporarily taken out of service in late 1993. It was stored for a short time at Fort Worth, Texas, and in 1994 joined ADC Airlines.

AERONAVES DEL PERU

This airline started life in 1965 as Compania de Aviacion Aeronaves del Peru, when former staff of the Peruvian Air Force started to operate a couple of Douglas DC-6 passenger piston liners. In 1970, a sole DC-7C turned the company's activities into pure cargo operations, until it was joined by two former RCAF Canadair CL-44-6 turboprops on regular cargo charters to Miami during the mid-1970s. In 1978, a Rolls-Royce Conway-powered former Alitalia aircraft arrived as a newly converted DC-8-43F dedicated jet freighter, dramatically speeding up international cargo services. During the early 1980s, Aeronaves del Peru significantly expanded its Douglas fleet with various models of the DC-8-41/43 and 50-passenger series. Two former Northwest Orient Airlines Boeing 707-351Cs joined the cargo operations of the early 1990s, while some of the DC-8 freighters had already been sold or had been taken out of service. Aeronaves del Peru discontinued its activities during summer 1994. A Douglas DC-8F-54 and a DC-8-61AF were reported to be stored at Baranquilla, Colombia, while both B-707-351Cs remain inactive and were parked at Lima during 1995.

The last Douglas DC-8F-54 in service with Aeronaves del Peru was OB-1300 *Santa Elena*, seen here at Frankfurt in July 1992. Before becoming a Peruvian freighter, the aircraft had spent its first sixteen years as one of eight DC-8-54Fs delivered to Air Canada in 1966. After two years of storage in the desert of Arizona, the aircraft was reactivated and passed through the hands of a couple of lessors in 1984, to be finally taken into service for less than a year by VIASA of Venezuela. Initially named *Santa Isidora*, the freighter was purchased by Aeronaves del Peru in early 1987, and logged further airborne hours on cargo flights throughout South America and to the USA. It was found stored in Colombia during the mid-1990s.

AFFRETAIR

Starting domestic passenger and ad hoc cargo charter operations within Rhodesia under the name of Air Trans Africa in 1966, the company's first two aircraft were a four-engined de Havilland DH 114 Heron 1B and a former Pan American World Airways Douglas DC-7C piston liner. 1972 was the year for a leap into the jet age when, in close co-operation with Air Gabon Cargo, a Seabord World Airlines Douglas DC-8F-55 was purchased, receiving the name *Situtunga*. A second DC-8F-55 was purchased from Air Gabon Cargo in 1975, TR-LVK, later to become Z-WSB. A large Canadair CL-44D4-2 turboprop freighter, TR-LVO, was acquired in 1975, temporarily leased to its Gabonese partner, to be flown by Affretair until 1980. As a result of the historical 'Lancaster House Conference' of 1979 in London, when the formal status of a republic was granted to Rhodesia, Affretair was introduced as the new corporate name. Both DC-8 Jet Traders became the backbone of the newly born National Cargo Airline of Zimbabwe, and were destined to operate into the last decade of the century. A third, and larger, Douglas DC-8-71F (AF) series with CFM56 engines was leased from GPA in June 1992; however, it was returned after two years. The company's regular and scheduled cargo operations of 1995 included a weekly trip across the Indian Ocean to Singapore, twice-weekly services to Johannesburg, Zimbabwe's largest African trading partner, and a flight to Gaborone in Botswana, in addition serving Dar es Salaam, Cairo and Kano and Lagos in Nigeria. European services to Amsterdam were augmented to four weekly flights, all of them being extended to London–Gatwick. Southbound flights departing England for Zimbabwe, included intermediate stops at Lilongwe, Malawi and Lusaka, Zambia twice a week.

Coming in to land at Amsterdam–Schiphol in spring 1995 is Z-WSB, one of Affretair's well-aged Douglas DC-8F-55s. After thirty years in operation since it was built, flight ZL08 arrived with a load of perishable products on a direct routing from Harare, the capital of Zimbabwe, more than 8,000 km away. The Jet Trader was sold to Air Gabon Cargo in 1975 to be leased to the later Affretair in 1976. It served there for twenty long years until it was damaged at Harare in February 1996. Its sister ship, Z-WMJ, built in 1966 and named *Captain Jack Malloch*, continued as the company's sole freighter. In 1996, only eleven African-certificated Douglas DC-8F series 50 freighter aircraft were based in or regularly visited Europe – these were the five DC-8F-55s of MK/Flash Airlines, three DC-8F-54s of African International Airways, two DC-8F-55 of Liberia World Airlines and the last remaining DC-8F-55 of Affretair.

AFRICAN AIRLINES INTERNATIONAL

Nairobi-based African Airlines International operated its first two Boeing 707-300Bs on passenger charters within Africa and to the Middle East during 1990, one of which was a leased series 321B, 5Y-AXW, and the second an owned 320B model, 5Y-AXM, named *Mandera*. A third all-passenger B-707-330B, 5Y-AXI *Isiolo*, was leased from Seagreen Air Transport in 1993. The first and sole freighter was 5Y-AXG, a Kenya-certificated B-707-321C on lease from Continental Cargo & Trade Services of Accra in Ghana which started to operate regular cargo charter services between Europe and Africa in late 1990. Following a C-Check overhaul in late 1994, re-registered 9G-ADM was flown to Amman and did not return until January 1995, since when it has occasionally been chartered by Royal Jordanian. 9G-ADM was renamed *Tayma* in 1995, maintaining flight operations out of Ostend, and well on its way to celebrating its thirtieth anniversary on 14 November 1997.

African Boeing 707-321C, 9G-ADM *Garissa*, announces its arrival with a black trail of smoke as it sinks down on Ostend on a windless afternoon in June 1993. The picture shows the former Pan Am Clipper *Western Continent* N459PA of 1967 returning from Keflavik, Iceland, in the characteristic style of most of the first-generation jet aircraft of the 1960s.

Fuelled up for a 4,300 km medium-range return flight to the edge of the polar circle, 9G-ADM climbs out of Ostend on a hot summer's morning in June 1993, with its callsign ACE 577 indicating an assignment carried out for Race Cargo Airlines. Named after a north-eastern Kenyan town, *Garissa* lifted a load of vegetables to Keflavik in Iceland. Seven hours later, a number of refrigerator trucks were already waiting for the freighter to return to Ostend, unloading Iceland's number one export, fresh salmon.

AIR AFRIQUE

Arising out of the post-colonial era of the early 1960s, Air Afrique was formed in March 1961 by the freshly independent West and Central African nations Benin, Burkina Faso, Cameroon, Central African Republic, Chad, Congo-Brazzaville, Gabon, Ivory Coast, Mauritania, Niger, Senegal and Togo. Scheduled services between the member states and to major points in Europe were established in co-operation with Air France and the UAT subsidy SODETRAF. The company's headquarters were located at Abidjan, the commercial and banking centre of the Ivory Coast. Intra-African operations started in June 1961 with a fleet of DC-3s, twelve Douglas DC-4s and one DC-6 piston liner. International services to Paris, Bordeaux, Nizza and Marseille followed later in the year with two leased Lockheed L-1649A Starliners of Air France. The first jet, a former UAT Douglas DC-8-53, became TU-TCA in 1963. Four further DC-8 purchases augmented the capacity, including another 53, two 32/33s and a first 55F series for dedicated freighter services to Paris. A Douglas DC-8-63CF carried out regular transatlantic cargo services between Dakar and New York

JFK from early 1970. Cameroon detached its operations from Air Afrique in 1971 and then Gabon in 1976. Mali became a new and later member. Air Afrique's Douglas DC-10-30 widebodies had already joined the fleet in 1973, and three aircraft of that type added their thirteen-ton underfloor cargo capability to the passenger payload on routings to Europe. During the 1980s, three Airbus A300B4-203s laid the base for a future fleet consisting mainly of European-manufactured aircraft. During this decade two Boeing B-727-200s and an all-cargo B-747-200F were operated on lease for several years. A Lockheed TriStar and a Boeing 737-300 were short-time leased in early 1990, and spring 1991 saw the arrival of the first Airbus A310-304, of which seven aircraft were introduced to the majority of multinational routes by 1996. An Antonov 12 and a B-737-200 combi were matched to low-density schedules within Africa. Between 1989 and 1993, four Boeing 707-320C freighters were subsequently leased to establish a frequent all-cargo network.

Arriving newly painted at Ostend Airport on 31 October 1991, Romanian flagged YR-ABN was the first of four Boeing 707-300C freighters to be operated by TAROM crews on behalf of Air Afrique. YR-ABM undershot the runway at Abidjan's Port Bouet Airport in January 1993, and the last flight of the pictured Boeing 707-321C, YR-ABN, ended in August 1995 while overshooting the runway at N'Djamena, Chad. The remaining sister ships YR-ABA and YR-ABC were the last Romanian-operated B-707-3K1Cs on Air Afrique's cargo network during 1995, joined by another couple of DAS Air Cargo B-707-320Cs which were contracted initially for two years.

AFRICAN INTERNATIONAL AIRWAYS

Associated with and managed by the Intavia Group of the UK, African International Airways started to build up a dedicated freighter fleet with three all-cargo configurated DC-8F-54s. Certificated in the small South African monarchy of Swaziland, a first Douglas DC-8F-55 Jet Trader was introduced in August 1985, specialising in supplementary contract services for major airlines such as Alitalia, providing their scheduled feeder cargo routes on an ACMI (Aircraft, Crew, Maintenance, Insurance) contract basis. The initial aircraft was sold to Nigerian Flash Airlines in 1987, while the fleet's second DC-8F-54, also registered 3D-ADV, entered the same year and was followed by two others in 1990 and 1992.

Just airborne from Frankfurt's runway 18 in April 1994 and on a scheduled, long-term contract charter for Alitalia, this passenger/cargo convertible aircraft was originally delivered to United Air Lines as N8046U in 1966. The DC-8F-54 remained in service in the US with Trans International Airlines and Connie Kalitta Services, before being purchased by African International as 3D-AFR in May 1990.

AIR GABON

The first widebody airliner to feature Air Gabon titles and a cheatline in national colours was a B-747-2B4B combi, OD-AGJ, leased from Middle East Airlines. Subsequently in 1978, Air Gabon received two of its own jets, a B-737-200C Advanced and a B-747-2Q2B (SCD) combi, that had a TR-LXK pre-delivery registration, which was changed to F-ODJG when it arrived in Gabon in July 1978, as the company's flagship *Leon M'ba*, named after the appointed President during the nation's independence from France in 1960. Two converted Vickers Vanguard short-range freighters were purchased by Air Gabon Cargo during the early 1980s, a V953C Merchantman and a V952F Cargoliner, both of which were sold to Intercargo Service at Paris–Orly in 1987, after a Lockheed L-100-30 Hercules had been phased into service earlier in 1985. The short- to medium-range fleet received a Fokker 100 in late 1989, and two Boeing 737-228 and 727-228 Advanced models were leased from Air France in 1993. Two seventy-seater Aérospatiale/Alenia ATR72-202 turboprops joined the regional network, which served twenty-two domestic points, including smaller airfields with the help of CASA 212 Aviocar STOL utility transports.

After an early-morning arrival from Gabon, the company's combi-freighter was pulled away from its parking stand at Paris Aerogare Terminal 1 in April 1990, to be loaded at the Charles de Gaulle/Air France Cargo Terminal on the southern side of the huge airport area. The B-747 combi has a capacity for fourteen ten-foot main-deck containers, allowing for a pure cargo payload of thirty-five tons, while 252 passengers are seated in the front. Whole ten-foot-high machines, or two-level car transportation units, can be accepted.

ROYAL AIR MAROC

Originating in 1953, Compagnie Cherifienne de Transport Aérien, operated Douglas DC-3s, DC-4s, and Sud-Ouest SO 30P Bretagne piston liners on domestic and international flights to Western Europe. With the establishment of the Kingdom of Morocco during the year of its independence in 1956, Mohammed V declared the above company as the national carrier. It resumed operations under its new name, Royal Air Maroc, in 1957, introducing a first Lockheed L-749A Constellation. The 1960s saw the initiation of a major fleet development, and with the Sud-Aviation Caravelle 3 already available, Royal Air Maroc became one of the very first customers for the elegant jetliner in 1960, ordering four more in 1968. Four L-749A Constellations were purchased between 1960 and 1962, of which two were successively converted into freighters. The 1970s were dominated by purchasing Boeing`s best-sellers. Two intercontinental B-707-320C convertibles commenced cargo and passenger services in early 1975 along with a new B-747-2B6 combi in September 1978. Two B-737-2B6Cs arrived in 1983, catering for flexible passenger/cargo services to capitals within medium range. A special performance B-747SP44 and two B-757-2B6 all-passenger aircraft rounded up the fleet structure during the mid-1980s. Three Aérospatiale/Alenia ATR42-300 turboprops were leased for domestic services in 1989, while the constantly growing Royal Air Maroc kept pace with the latest developments by inaugurating the sophisticated Boeing 737-400 and 500 series by the early 1990s. A Boeing 747-428 was acquired in October 1993, when the B-747SP44 was sold.

CN-RME, Boeing 737-2B6C, arriving at Frankfurt in January 1991 as flight AT926 from Agadir and Tangier. Conversion into the all-cargo version of the 200C Advanced variant, which is capable of carrying about fifteen tons of payload, takes a couple of hours and was practised after the day's completed passenger schedules. Purchased during 1983, the company's pair of B-737 convertibles carried out the dedicated cargo programme exclusively on the non-stop routes between Morocco and Europe.

AIR ZAIRE

Traditionally, Zaire was a good customer of the Californian Douglas Aircraft Corporation. After independence from the Belgian colonial administration in 1961, Air Congo took over DC-3, DC-4 and DC-6 piston liners from SABENA. The first jet was a leased B-707 in 1963, which was substituted by two former Pan American DC-8-32/33 passenger aircraft in June 1969. Two DC-8-63AF/CFs marked the start of an ambitious fleet development plan in the early seventies. The Douglas Super Sixties were followed by two McDonnell Douglas DC-10-30 widebodies in 1973 and 1974, while at the same time three Boeing B-737-298C convertibles entered service on domestic and international flights to West and Central African capitals, along with four Fokker F-27-600 turboprops fitted with a side-cargo door. A former Pan American B-747-121, N747QC *Clipper America*, was leased for more than a year from late 1973. Since then, the country's economic situation has steadily worsened. One DC-10-30, 9Q-CLT, was sold to British Caledonian Airways in 1985, as well as one of the B-737-200C short-haulers. Both DC-8-63AF/CF aircraft were sold beween 1990-1992, and the last DC-10-30 flagship, 9Q-CLI, handled the European long-haul schedules linking Lubumbashi and Kinshasa on three weekly flights with Brussels, including Paris–CDG twice, and Rome–Fiumicino once a week until being withdrawn from use soon after. With the deterioration of world market prices for copper and cobalt in 1971, Zaire's foreign debt rose constantly to astronomical heights and the country's situation dramatically headed into an economical and political collapse. A relaunch of Air Zaire's international schedules to Europe under a new name with a leased Airbus A310-200 is intended by Belgium's carrier SABENA during 1996, in league with Swiss and South African investors.

This DC-8F-54 started a late career with Air Zaire as 9Q-CLV in spring 1992, when it left its previous owner Connie Kalitta Services as N803CK, exchanged in a deal for a DC-8-63CF, 9Q-CLG, which was too large for Air Zaire's merely domestic and continental passenger and cargo operations of the 1990s. Parked at the Brucargo centre at Brussels–Zaventem in September 1992, 9Q-CLV was by far the oldest species of first-generation cargo aircraft on flights to Europe. Delivered to Trans Canada Air Lines in January 1961, and still configured as a passenger DC-8-42/43 fitted with Rolls-Royce Conway RCo.12 bypass engines, it was converted into a passenger/cargo convertible freighter in 1978, paying a first visit to the piston city Detroit when flying for Zantop International Airlines, re-engined with Pratt & Whitney JT3D turbofans. Kalitta acquired this Jet Trader as N803CK in 1987, until it was sold to Air Zaire in early 1992.

AIR ALGERIE

The name Air Algerie first appeared with the merger of two local French colonial airlines, Compagnie de Transport Aérien of 1947 and Compagnie Air Transport joining forces during May 1953. A fleet of ten Douglas C-54A/Bs and Lockheed L-749A Constellations was developed, until in December 1959 the first of five SE 210 Caravelles inaugurated scheduled passenger jetservices out of the capital Algiers to Paris. Eight years later, four former Lufthansa Convair 440s were purchased and converted into CV 640s during 1968. Since the early 1970s, and after becoming a government-owned airline in 1972, the international network of short- to medium-range destinations rapidly expanded with the gradual introduction of eleven Boeing 727-200 and B-737-200 Advanced models. The cargo division was established in 1981 when three new Lockheed L-100-30 Hercules freighters started flying scheduled flights, linking Algiers, Oran, Constantine and Annaba as the largest cities in the coastal Algerian region with European capitals. Four Airbus A310-203s were chosen as widebodies to operate high-density routes to Paris, as well as to Cairo, Damascus and Jeddah, especially during the Haj season. Three 250-seater Boeing 767-300s were the latest entries in 1990, serving Paris–Orly on four daily flights throughout the year.

On final approach to Frankfurt in summer 1993 is Air Algerie's third Lockheed L-100-30, 7T-VHL, arriving on a twice-weekly non-stop northbound cargo schedule from Algiers. The stretched commercial Hercules proved the ideal aircraft for the North African carrier's purposes, satisfying the domestic oil industry's tough demands for an aircraft capable of transporting a large variety of oil exploration supplies and vehicles. Fully loaded with a payload of twenty-three tons, the L-100-30 could easily reach Frankfurt, London–Heathrow, Paris–Orly and Brussels on its non-stop three- to four-hour flight-time. Delivered in 1981, two freighters remained as the flying backbone of the cargo fleet in 1995, while 7T-VHK was damaged during an emergency landing in central Sahara at Tamanrasset near the Hoggar Mountains in 1989.

TAAG ANGOLA AIRLINES

Founded on the initiative of the Portuguese government in 1938, Direccão Exploracão dos Transportes Aereos, which was the source of the later-used three-letter designator DTA, became the body responsible for the development of air transport in Angola. Three de Havilland DH 89A Dragon Rapides were the company's first aircraft to start flying along the coast and into the highlands of this large southern African country in July 1940. In 1945, three Douglas DC-3s joined the small fleet and gave long service of more than twenty years. Two convertible Boeing B-737-2M2Cs became the first jet aircraft to operate with TAAG Angola Airlines in 1975 when the red and orange livery was introduced on both aircraft. Designed by Albano Neves e Sousa, the tail-fin logo featured the 'Palança Negra', an extremely rare species of antelope found only in Angola. With a road and rail network ruined by the ever-raging civil war, air transport claimed a superior role calling for the rugged L-100-20 and -30 Hercules. Two Ilyushin 62Ms were introduced in 1986/87 for services to Cuba. In 1990, the intercontinental passenger network welcomed a Lockheed TriStar 500 (CS-TEC), leased from Air Portugal. Flying in the full TAAG colours, the widebody linked Luanda with European destinations. In addition, the 250-seat TriStar served Johannesburg and Rio de Janeiro. An extensive domestic scheduled network, carried out by the F-27s and B-737s, had already spread to serve twenty-two destinations.

D2-TOJ was one of TAAG's first convertible Boeing 707-349Cs which helped to develop the intercontinental passenger and cargo network from Luanda. Contrary to the bilateral English titles applied on aircraft of the subsidy Angola Air Charter, black port side letters introduced this carrier in the Portuguese language as Linhas Aereas de Angola. Based at Ostend during the early 1990s, D2-TOJ did not receive hush-kits like its sister ships due to an incident at Luanda in February 1992.

From a total of eleven Boeing 707-300Cs and one B-707-382B delivered to TAAG between 1977 and 1993, seven convertible freighters were transferred to its subsidy Angola Air Charter, who have operated worldwide ad hoc and scheduled cargo services since 1987. Pictured in spring 1990, the flight-log of D2-TOG recorded the B-707-373C's 1,000th flight from Luanda to its European base of operations in Belgium, and it was therefore named *City of Ostend*. Leased by TAAG since 1978, D2-TOG was returned to its lessor in summer 1991, when after a service life of twenty-seven years its very last flight ended at Kent International Airport at Manston, where the freighter was broken up for spares together with its sister ship D2-TOU.

Seen leaving the runway is Angola Air Charter's D2-TOK, B-707-324C at Ostend Airport. The completely revised livery was first introduced on a company's B-737-200 in 1993, and D2-TOK was the only hush-kit-equipped B-707 bearing these colours that has been spotted in Europe.

COMPAGNIE NATIONALE NAGANAGANI
(BURKINA FASO)

Formerly a French protectorate, the African Sahel-state of Upper Volta became independent in 1960 and was renamed Burkina Faso in 1984. The republic suffers from infertile land and devastating droughts, circumstances which make massive food imports inevitable. During 1984, Compagnie Nationale Naganagani was formed to operate the government's Boeing 707-336C registered XT-ABX. It flew unscheduled flights from the capital Ouagadougou in a variety of configurations combining roles as cargo or passenger transport, as well as being the presidential aircraft. The convertible freighter was one of only two jets in the national aviation register. A second B-707-321B 'XT-ABZ', was purchased from the French Point Air, which had ceased operations during March 1987. As a member of Air Afrique, Burkina Faso's international cargo services continued to be flown by the carrier's B-707-320Cs on weekly scheduled services, as well as by the lower-hold capacities of scheduled Airbus A310 and McDonnell Douglas DC-10-30s. XT-BBF was leased for only a few months during 1989 as the fleet's third aircraft.

The swallow, a widespread bird of passage flying way south to the Black Continent, is placed on the fin of this Boeing 707-328C 'XT-BBF' wearing the old cheatlines of ZAS Airline of Egypt. Heavily loaded for a non-stop return leg to its Ouagadougou base, the airline's three-letter ICAO designation 'BFN' was standing for Burkina Faso Naganagani. In late 1989, the freighter was flagged in Switzerland, operating sub-charters for a number of scheduled airlines on flights out of Europe to Africa as HB-IEI of Homac Aviation, to join Avistar Airlines as 5B-DAZ since mid-1992.

CAIRO CHARTER & CARGO

The foundation of Cairo Charter & Cargo as a new Egyptian passenger and freight airline in late 1991 resulted from a privatisation programme initiated by the government to lower the nation's foreign debt and budget deficit. The aircraft inherited were two medium-range Tupolev 154M passenger jets, and two Ilyushin 76TD long-range freighters. The 160-seat Tupolev 154Ms plunged into service at the beginning of summer 1992. Everything went well until Islamic fundamentalists stirred up some trouble that heavily shook the Egyptian tourist industry: a terrorist shotgun attack on a sightseeing bus resulted in the first victims among European holiday-makers in autumn 1992. The aftermath of this and subsequent events directly harmed the profile of Cairo Charter & Cargo, and they found themselves cut off from earning profit on their trunk routes to destinations in the Nile Valley. Affected by this unpredictable recession, the complete fleet of Cairo Charter & Cargo ceased operations early that year and was taken over by the Iranian Mahan Air, based at Kerman.

SU-OAC, one of two Tupolev 154Ms of Cairo Charter & Cargo, is seen departing Frankfurt during its first and last summer of passenger services between Europe and Egypt in July 1992. Available since 1982, and re-engined with Aviadvigatel D-30KU-154-II turbofans, the M version was freshly delivered from the Russian Tupolev Design Bureau at Samara only four months previously, improved to give a smoother take-off and a more economical four-hour cruise to its destinations of Luxor or Hurghada. Though not a freighter, the 100-ton-class aircraft also used the black Cargo suffix that was painted on the company's forty-ton payload Ilyushin 76TD sister ships. Approximately 150 of 200 produced Tu-154Ms were exported to operators outside Russia; the production number of all the marks was assumed to have reached 900. The eighteen-wheeled tri-jet could haul a maximum load of up to 180 passengers and the cargo of five belly compartments, each of thirty-nine cubic metres, over a distance of 3,900 km.

CAMEROON AIRLINES

Established in 1953, Air Cameroon was a founding member of Air Afrique in 1961, the year of its complete independence, flying a couple of DC-4s. Like Gabon, Cameroon also decided to withdraw from the multinational airline consortium, and with the help of Air France as a major shareholder, Cameroon Airlines came into being in November 1971 offering international passenger and cargo services out of the largest city and the country's industrial centre Douala with further DC-4s and a French-registered B-707-328. The first owned B-707-3H7C, TJ-CAA, was delivered in late 1972, together with two B-737-2H7C convertibles for the domestic and West African market. Primarily an agricultural country, Cameroon was earning a good deal of money from oil exports, and could afford to operate a B-747-2H7B combi flagship, delivered in 1981. Two HS 748-2As were introduced on the domestic network during 1982. In 1995, the intra-African network of B-737 services ranged from Abidjan along the West African coast throughout Central Africa to Nairobi and Kigali in the east, and Harare. Weekly B-747 combi schedules for the Muslim population of more than twenty per cent were maintained to Jeddah, as well as to neighbouring Lagos and Kinshasa, and to Johannesburg. Four weekly B-747 combi flights from Douala to Paris–Orly were carried out on two non-stop services, while one rotation was extended to London–Gatwick, including Brussels since 1996.

Named after the national symbol, the 4,070m high Mont Cameroun, TJ-CAB, the company's Boeing 747-2H7B combi, is rolling for the holding point of runway 07 at Paris–Orly during the summer of 1989. The combi's side-cargo door is clearly visible in the aft upper deck.

DAS AIR CARGO

This is the trading name for the all-cargo airline activities of the Ugandan company Dairo Air Services, founded in 1983. Operations started with a B-707-338C, registered 5N-ARQ, leased from GAS Air Cargo in January 1984 for ad hoc cargo charter flights between Africa and Europe. Scheduled part charter services were started in 1985 following the appointment of ANA Aviation Services to provide cargo sales and commercial management. With the delivery of a further three freighters in 1993, a fleet of four fully hush-kitted B-707-320C all-cargo freighters was offering worldwide ad hoc full charters, as well as scheduled cargo services to sixteen cities in East, Southern and West Africa. Because of its outstanding and frequent services offered to a wide range of clients, including horticultural producers in Africa flying their fresh fruit, flowers and vegetables directly into Europe, DAS Air Cargo was voted 'Best All-Cargo Airline in 1993' by *Air Cargo News*. The company commenced operating a DC-10-30F aircraft, 5X-JOE, in November 1995 and planned to introduce a second aircraft. An agreement was signed with Air Afrique to operate two B-707F aircraft until mid-1997 for their operations between Europe and Africa.

5N-ARQ, Boeing 707-338C, climbs steeply out at Ostend Airport on a ferry flight to London–Gatwick. The aircraft regularly brings in thirteen pallets and full belly holds of pineapples. Flights to Entebbe, Dar es Salaam, Djibouti and Lusaka in East and Southern Africa normally route back to Europe via Nairobi. From September to May, the Nairobi services were increased to at least four weekly flights to carry thirty-three-ton payloads of flowers to Amsterdam or Rotterdam via Cairo for a technical stop.

EGYPT AIR

With a history dating back to 1932 the carrier eventually became Egypt Air in 1971. Between 1968 and 1975, the company's fleet politics were influenced by President Nasser's skilful strategy of using the rivalry between Russian and American manufacturers. It purchased the first of seven Boeing 707-366Cs, as well as Ilyushin 18s, Antonov 24 turboprops and Tupolev 154s medium-range jets. President Sadat continued to encourage the fleet's redevelopment by adding new B-737-266s in 1976. Since then, Western-type widebodies have been favoured and Airbus A300B4s and Boeing B-767-266ERs were purchased between 1980 and 1984, plus the leasing of a first B-747-200. A slightly redesigned corporate livery was introduced on two new B-747-366 combis in summer 1988. From that time on, and as it was a worldwide custom, the rivalry between the Airbus and Boeing manufacturing plants was used to gain better prices, with three B-767-366ERs acquired in 1989 followed by nine A300B4-622Rs, five B-737-566s and seven A320-231s by 1993. Two A340-300s were leased from Gulf Air in summer 1995, Egypt Air having ordered three Airbus A340-200s with a further two options. Boeing received orders for three B-777-200s for delivery in 1997, which will appear in the company's new corporate design.

SU-GAM *Cleopatra*, taxies to the holding point of Paris–Orly's runway 25 on a twice-weekly schedule from Cairo to New York–JFK in May 1989. It was introduced as the second Boeing 747-366 combi flagship in June 1988, Egypt Air being the first Arabian airline to introduce this model.

ETHIOPIAN AIRLINES

Proclaimed as the national carrier by Emperor Haile Selassie, Ethiopian Airlines started in 1946. From its early years, and with the assistance of TWA, Ethiopian Airlines developed both a complex internal route system and one of the biggest African networks with the continent's largest fleet of Douglas DC-3s. During the 1950s three Convair 240s, and later in the decade, three Douglas DC-6B freighters, opened routes via Sudan to Ghana and Liberia and to Nigeria during the early 1960s, while flights to Athens had been extended to Frankfurt in 1958. With TWA's long-term support effective until 1970, one of the important objectives included the future participation of this major African airline in the expanding air cargo business of the early 1970s. The first couple of convertible B-707-320Cs were acquired during 1968, taking over the freight work of the DC-6Bs. Douala, Paris–Orly, London–Heathrow, Shanghai and Beijing were included in the network. The early 1980s were marked by a phase of modernisation with the introduction of three B-727-260 Advanced and two DHC-5A Buffalos, and in May 1984 Ethiopian Airlines became the first African airline to operate the Boeing B-767, using two models of the 260ER extended-range version capable of carrying an underfloor cargo load of twelve tons. Since 1987, a fleet of three was serving high-density destinations within Africa and the long-range routes to Europe, Beijing and Bangkok. Short-haul operations from smaller airfields improved with the delivery of two Lockheed L-100-30 Hercules during 1988. In 1990, Ethiopian Airlines led the way to become the first operator of the Boeing B-757-260PF freighter in Africa. In 1995 Ethiopian's freighter fleet consisted of one B-707-327C, one 757-260PF, two L-100-30s and the belly holds of three B-767s, two B-727s, four B-757s and one B-737.

Demonstrating a STOL performance after a take-off run of fewer than 1,000 metres, departing Frankfurt on a cargo charter flight in April 1994, is ET-AKG of Ethiopian Airlines. Having taken delivery of two brand-new Lockheed L-100-30 Hercules freighters in 1988, ET-AKG entered in December 1992 as a third model on lease from the Ministry of Transport, replacing ET-AJL which had crashed south of Djibouti in September 1991. The versatility of this Super Hercules included the capability of transporting a maximum payload of 23.5 tons as far as 3,400 km, as well as landing on airstrips not longer than 1,500m. All features derived from the legendary C-130, tactical troop transport aircraft, continuously manufactured since 1955. More than 2,000 Hercules have been built in many versions during thirty-five years, while the line production still continues during the mid nineties.

ET-AJS, Ethiopian Cargo's sole Boeing B-757-260PF package freighter, completes a 180-degree turn in the loop of runway 26 at Ostend, Belgium during May 1992. With the delivery of this type of freighter, powered by two Pratt & Whitney PW 2040 engines in August 1990, Ethiopian Airlines became the first B-757PF operator outside the USA. Capable of carrying a maximum payload of nearly thirty-three tons, the aircraft can haul twenty-two tons over a distance of 7,200 km.

FLASH AIRLINES

Founded by Chief P.E. Osakwe in 1985, Flash Airlines entered Nigeria's air cargo market as one of the country's fully dedicated freight operators, offering worldwide cargo charter services. The first of two DC-8F-55 Jet Traders was leased from the Intavia Group of the UK and had its registration changed from 3D-ADV to 5N-ATY in 1987. Sister ship 5N-ATZ appeared at European Airports in early 1988, displaying larger blue Flash Airlines titles and an enlarged corporate tail-fin logo. The fluctuating ad hoc air cargo market out of Europe often did not provide a continuous demand for the old forty-ton-class jet freighters, and the company's aircraft stayed on the ground at their Ostend base for many days. Availability at short notice, however, was the strength of such a carrier, provided that the aircraft were serviceable and ready. During the early 1990s, Flash Airlines' corporate identity disappeared and the fleet was reduced to one aircraft. 5N-ATZ was jointly operated with MK Air Cargo of the UK, bringing its rich Nigerian connections and African experience into the alliance. During the mid-1990s, all five Douglas DC-8F-55s of the renamed MK Airlines were jointly operated by Flash Airlines' flight crews.

'Tango Zulu', the second Flash Airlines DC-8F-55, 5N-ATZ, returns to its European base at Ostend Airport from a lucrative three-day cross-Africa contract cargo charter on behalf of Air Zaire in April 1991. The part-shipment round trip departed Belgium for Lagos, Nigeria, continued to Kinshasa and Lubumbashi in Zaire and to Harare in Zimbabwe, to return northbound to Europe via Cairo, Egypt. The original freighter was the sole DC-8F-55 in service with Iberia, Lineas Aereas de España, for more than seventeen non-hush-kit years between 1968 and 1985, flying the large domestic network between the Spanish mainland, the Mediterranean and Canary Islands as well as international routes. Receiving its noise suppressors from Miami's Quiet Nacelle Corporation soon after, the aircraft returned to Europe and appeared in the striking classic colours of Flash Airlines in early 1988. Sold to a lessor in late 1992, the titles of 5N-ATZ were erased from the fuselage. Acquired by MK Air Cargo in January 1995, the freighter took up services in the full colours of MK Airlines between Europe, Nigeria and other African destinations, re-registered as 9G-MKD in October 1995.

FOREMOST AVIATION (NIGERIA) LTD

Foremost Aviation was founded by Chief Adeosun in 1992 to feed the demand of the estimated 10 million inhabitants of Lagos for air-freighted import shipments. The first and only freighter to bear the company's trading name and logo was the Nigerian-registered Boeing 707-351C, 5N-JIL, being leased from Omega Air since October 1992. The aircraft already had a Nigerian history, which started after it flew seven years for Northwest Orient Airlines from 1965 and then nine years for Cathay Pacific Airways from 1972. It commenced services on lease to Nigeria Airways in summer 1982. In 1983, the aircraft received its original 5N-ASY identification and the livery of Lagos-based UAS Cargo (United Air Service). On lease to EAS Cargo Airlines (Executive Aviation Services) from late 1987, the 707 was repainted and featured another remarkable African corporate design. After serving a short time for the Ugandan Dairo Air Service (DAS Air Cargo) in summer 1992, the aircraft was purchased in October by the Irish lessor Omega Air,

and was delivered to Foremost Aviation to participate in the big business of the winter season, importing perishables from Africa to Europe. An operational base was maintained at Ostend, Belgium, and a corporate headquarters office at Feltham, near London–Heathrow. The operational profile of 5N-JIL included missions to Africa for humanitarian organisations such as Medecins Sans Frontières, or by Race Cargo Airlines for flights to Accra, Ghana, importing pineapples and fruits. The aircraft was also wet-leased to Heavylift Cargo Airlines, and last but not least flew a series of contract charters on behalf of the Zairean government, shipping loads of President Mobutu's freshly printed new currency from Munich to Kinshasa. After a year of active presence, 5N-JIL was returned to the lessor in October 1994 and transferred to the Honduran aviation register, to be leased to the South African Impala Air Cargo of Johannesburg.

Awaiting its palletised load at Ostend Airport in June 1993, pictured is Foremost Aviation's one and only B-707-351C freighter, 5N-JIL, named *The Latter Rain*, prior to its departure under Nigerian Captain Benson. Mentioned in brackets below the titles is KATI AIR, which is the abbreviation for Kano Transport International Ltd, who have an interest in the Foremost Aviation venture.

GAS AIR CARGO

General and Aviation Services Limited was founded as a Nigerian family concern in 1973 with its headquarters located at Ikeja, next to Murtala Mohammed Airport, Lagos. Scheduled domestic services were started in late 1975 with BAC 1-11s leased from the Romanian carrier TAROM. The first used Boeing 707-338C freighter was 5N-ARQ, inaugurating regular international air cargo services out of Lagos to East Africa and Europe in 1983. In the same year, Entebbe-based Ugandan company Dairo Air Services was formed to operate ad hoc charter flights to Europe leasing 5N-ARQ from early 1984. In 1987 the operation of GAS Air Express Ltd was conducted out of the company's London office, comprising air freight services with a subchartered, former Pan American B-707-321C, 5N-AWO, out of Ostend Airport in Belgium. The need for a second aircraft led to the lease of 5N-AYJ, a B-707-351C which was still sporting the livery of its previous operator Biman Bangladesh Airlines; it was in service from June 1988 until six months later when it crashed south of Luxor, Egypt. Services between Europe and Nigeria were kept up with the remaining aircraft, 5N-AWO, until it disappeared from the scene in early 1991, being parked and withdrawn from use at Lagos. In April 1992, 9G-RBO, a former Northwest Orient Airlines B-707-351C, was chartered from EAS Cargo Airlines. Based at Ostend, the aircraft was damaged during an emergency belly landing with retracted landing gears at Llorin, Nigeria, some 250 km short of reaching Lagos, leading to the termination of GAS Air Cargo operations to Europe.

Looking the worse for wear, the scars of time and hard work had found their place on the paint finish of GAS Air Express Ltd Boeing B-707-321C, 5N-AWO. Cleared for take-off by Ostend Tower in February 1991, the former *Clipper Eagle* N462PA, delivered to Pan American Airlines in 1967, was keeping the brakes on while running up the power of the four non-hush-kit Pratt & Whitney JT3D-3B engines. A few months later, the certificate of airworthiness was withdrawn after aviation authority inspectors had registered maintenance deficiencies. Owing to the solid and unharmed airframe of this Boeing 707, it eventually reappeared at Luxembourg in April 1993 fit for service with Imperial Cargo Airlines of Ghana. It was owned by Alpine Air prior to being sold to Azerbaijan Airlines in 1996.

IMPALA AIR

With its headquarters at Johannesburg, South Africa, Air Charter Services Ltd. was established as a company in 1992 trading as Impala Air, named after the continent's famous antelope. The first owned aircraft in operation was a Boeing 707-351C freighter, leased from the Omega Air Honduras division as HR-AME. The twenty-eight-year-old aircraft was handed over in October 1993 featuring two doves in the tail fin rising over a script reading 'Peace in our land'. A former Trans World Airlines Lockheed L-1011 TriStar 1, which appeared in basic Air Sweden colours with large Impala Air South Africa titles painted on the upper fuselage, was leased for a few months during 1994. After flying passenger charters out of Johannesburg to the 2,000 islands of the Republic of Maldives in the Indian Ocean, the widebody was returned to the Swedish TriStar operator Air Operations of Europe (Air Ops) as SE-DPV. In May 1994 the B-707-351C was handed back to the lessor, and as a substitution for the cargo operations, ex-Europe, Impala Air Cargo leased a second B-707-347C in September 1994, registered 9J-AFT, which never appeared in the same livery as HR-AMA. The aircraft received its ZS-NLJ South African registration when it was bought by Impala Air Cargo in January 1995, and operated in co-operation with Orchid Aviation. HR-AME, meanwhile, had also ceased to fly for the company after having completed its South American adventure and being grounded without engines at the capital Brasilia. It finally returned to the Irish used aircraft leasing and finance company Omega Air during summer 1995.

Boeing 707-351C, HR-AME, has been leased by Impala Air since September 1993. The hush-kitted freighter can be seen rolling to its last take-off from Ostend Airport on behalf of Impala Air Cargo in mid-May 1994, to be returned afterwards to the lessor Omega Air, who leased the aircraft to Transbrasil without changing the livery.

KABO AIR

Kano-based Kabo Air was one of the large private Nigerian airlines whose primary business was founded on scheduled domestic passenger flights within Nigeria. In 1981, five second-hand Sud Aviation Caravelle SE210s were acquired. In 1987 three B-727-25s joined the fleet, and during the following year the company entered the intercontinental jet freight market with a passenger DC-8-55 of 1965 vintage. This was ferried across the Atlantic to Florida where a conversion into a DC-8-55F was carried out at Opa Locka. At the same time, the freighter was fitted with hush kits to meet the European noise reduction requirements. Named *Sir Amandu Bello*, the aircraft was soon contracted on charters out of the European Benelux countries, regularly operating out of Luxembourg on behalf of the worldwide freight forwarder Transalpina. In February 1992, Kabo Air Cargo leased a B-707- 321C, 5N-MAS, from Trans Air Services, which lost two engines en route to Nigeria over France and was forced to land at Istres near Marseille. During the early 1990s, Kabo Air abruptly enlarged its domestic fleet with thirteen BAe (BAC) 1-11-200s and 400s, delivered from England between 1991 and 1993. The One-Eleven was very much appreciated by Nigerian pilots because of its compactness and structural strength, proving its good design on daily schedules. With the arrival of a B-727-C3 and ten B-727-200s between 1992 and 1995, Kabo Air developed the country's second largest independent passenger fleet after Okada Air. The company's sole dedicated cargo DC-8-55F, 5N-AWE, was sold in 1994 to Over-Night Cargo Ltd, another Nigerian charter operator from Lagos.

Sir Amandu Bello of Kabo Air, parked on the main apron of Luxembourg Airport, shimmering after a spring shower in 1991. Manufactured as an original DC-8-55 version for up to 189 passengers, the aircraft operated out of Northern Europe from 1965, when it was delivered to Scandinavian Airlines System as SE-DBD *Folke Viking*. In 1982 the blue cheatline of Icelandair decorated the aircraft, and after conversion the DC-8-55F freighter's tail was painted showing the logo of Kabo Air in 1988.

In 1992 Kabo Air's DC-8-55F was repainted in a new livery with three narrow blue stripes running along the fuselage between larger red Kabo Air Cargo titles. A black sticker was placed adjacently showing a six-pointed star topped by the words 'African Star'. 5N-AWE is shown taking to the air at Ostend Airport in September 1993, shipping a consignment of fresh lettuce and vegetables to Iceland; it would return with salmon, a routing that became a weekly task for MK Airlines, which was to welcome the aircraft into their fleet in 1995 as 9G-MKE. Visible is the right-hand air intake under the nose. The fast air flow generates a turbo compressor which feeds the flight deck and main cabin with fresh air – vital for livestock transportation.

KATALE AERO TRANSPORT

In 1978, the owner of a huge Zairean coffee plantation called Domaine de Katale, founded his own airline of the same name. It started operations with a Bristol Britannia 252C flying out of Goma. Up until 1984 a fleet of six Britannias of the 252C/253C and 312F series that had served with the British Royal Air Force, British Overseas Airways Corporation and later many other cargo companies, and also a single Canadair CL-44-6 from the Royal Canadian Air Force, lifted the black gold from Goma to Kinshasa and Mombasa, the Kenyan port on the Indian Ocean. Here the coffee sacks were loaded into vessels for worldwide export. During the early 1980s, when coffee prices dropped rapidly, the cargo company was forced to restructure its operations and fly general cargo on domestic and international charters. For this purpose, a Boeing 707-329C was purchased from the Belgian airline SABENA in 1983. It was registered 9Q-CVG and bore the

new title of Katale Aero Transport. This aircraft was implemented on African routes and replaced the Britannias on international charter flights to Europe. In March 1990 this aircraft was damaged beyond repair when a Belgian pilot undershot Goma's runway. The airline was now left with a single Douglas DC-8-55F, 9Q-CVH, introduced to the company in 1988 to carry out the freight work. Named *Hubert*, the remaining cargojet continued to fly for Katale until September 1991 when it was ferried to Ostend to avoid damage during a period of political unrest in Zaire. This flight ended the history of Katale Aero Transport. The DC-8 was grounded at Ostend until May 1992 when the aircraft was sold to Kinshasa-based operator New ACS. The Zairean Transair Cargo acquired the freighter in May 1993, occasionally flying non-hush-kitted services to Ostend in 1994, but in that December it was sold to Colombia.

An icy layer covers the sole Douglas DC-8-55F jet freighter, 9Q-CVH, of Zairean Katale Aero Transport seen grounded at Ostend during winter 1991/92. The freighter had been flying since 1966, first for Capitol International Airways and then Seaboard World Airlines, both American carriers, until 1974. It went on to fly for the independent French carriers UTA and SFAIR until 1988, then started freight charter work from its East African base Goma. It was eventually transferred to Colombia where it became active with Ibero Americana de Carga.

AIR MADAGASCAR

Air Madagascar, the national airline of the Malagasy Republic, was formed in 1962, four years after declaring independence. With a piston liner fleet of six Douglas DC-3s and five DHC-6 Twin Otters, an extemely dense domestic intra-island network was developed. The DC-3s were replaced by a total of five Nord 262s, serving between 1968 and 1975. Four Hawker Siddeley HS748s joined the fleet in 1980, two of which were fitted with side-cargo doors for combi services. Most of these were still operating together with the Twin Otters during the mid-1990s, linking fifty-eight domestic destinations within a vast network. With France as the biggest trading partner, Air Madagascar entered intercontinental jet services to Europe by serving Paris and Marseille in 1964 with a leased Boeing B-707-328. In 1979 the company's passenger and cargo revenue was boosted with the arrival of their sole B-747-2B2B combi, 5R-MFT. Making extensive use of the combi's mixed passenger/cargo configuration on northbound return flights to Paris, 5R-MFT departed Antananarivo's Ivato Airport on course to Nairobi and initially to Marseille, Djibouti, Rome and Jeddah, to reach its French main destination. In 1995, Air Madagascar's flagship *Tolom Piavotana* began to collect additional cargo at East Africa's freight hub in Nairobi, before continuing on to Paris–Charles de Gaulle.

Flagship 5R-MFT comes in at Zürich–Kloten in summer 1992 on the weekly evening flight arriving from Paris, to continue via Nairobi to Antananarivo. Air Madagascar was the second African company to start B-747-200 combi services to Europe in 1979.

MERCHANT EXPRESS AVIATION

Having placed its single Boeing 707-338C into the air cargo market between Europe and Africa in October 1994, the Nigerian newcomer from Lagos soon earned its reputation as a reliable and well organised company. Flying ad hoc sub-charter services for several customers out of Ostend, including the Department of Humanitarian Affairs of the United Nations, Merchant Express Aviation was contracted to operate on scheduled routings of the Ugandan DAS Air Cargo, operationally based at London–Gatwick.

5N-MXX was photographed in its initial livery in April 1995. Leased from the Aviation Leasing Group Inc (ALGI) of Kansas City, Missouri, 5N-MXX entered its thirtieth service year in late August 1995, after being the seventh of thirty-six B-707-323Cs delivered to American Airlines between 1963 and 1968. Since 1973, and for over sixteen years, it flew for the Brazilian VARIG as PP-VLP, and retained its cheatline when joining Buffalo Airways as N108BV in late 1989.

NIGERIA AIRWAYS

Two years before independence from Britain in 1960, Nigeria Airways was formed to take over the national services of West African Airways Corporation operating with a Britannia 102 leased from BOAC. A de Havilland Comet 4 was the first jet of the newly government-owned airline in January 1962. The 1970s saw a radical change from an economy primarily exporting agricultural products into a nation dominating the continent as Africa's wealthiest and OPEC's fifth largest oil-producing member. During this period, Nigeria Airways received its first convertible Boeing 707-3F9C, 5N-ABJ. Between 1976 and 1978, two Douglas DC-10-30 widebodies, two Boeing 727-2F9s and a third B-707-3F9C met the increased domestic and international capacity demand of a huge and diversified population of 100 million. Nigeria's 1995 domestic network of a dozen destinations was served by B-737-2F9s and partly by A310-222 out of Lagos, serving also the neighbouring West African capitals Abidjan, Accra, Banjul, Cotounou, Douala and Lome. Two A310-222s were serving Jeddah, Kinshasa, Libreville and London–Heathrow on four weekly flights, while a fifth rotation to the last European destination was carried out by a DC-10-30.

Performing a rolling take-off out of the turning loop of Ostend Airport in March 1990, the full blast of Nigeria Airways 5N-ABK, Boeing 707-3F9C *Olumo Rock*, cleared the runway of a layer of sand blown from the dunes of the nearby Belgian coast. With the secondary inlet doors of the four Pratt & Whitney JT3D-3B turbofans opened, additional air was drawn in to provide an increased jet intake and thrust development.

Featuring a 'Flying Elephant' framed between the green-white-green national flag of Nigeria, the company's classical symbol was later replaced by an eagle painted on all of the fleet's aircraft. Delivered straight from the line into a Nigeria flooded by oil revenues in early 1973, 5N-ABK was the second of a total of three convertible passenger/cargo Boeing 707s.

OVERNIGHT CARGO LTD

In May 1993, Ikoyi, based at Lagos as Overnight Cargo Ltd and Vital Link Aviation (Consultants) Ltd of the UK arranged to sub-lease a B-707-351C from Buffalo Airways. After the neutralisation of the vertical fin, the remnant of a Heavylift Cargo Airlines cheatline gave evidence of the freighter's prior identity, having operated for the British cargo specialist out of London–Stansted from March 1989 until March 1990. For Overnight Cargo Ltd, the jet flew a number of charter operations out of Ostend from September 1993, taking advantage of its 5N-OCL identification on flights to Nigeria. Simultaneously, a former Flash Airlines DC-8F-55, 5N-ATZ, was leased until late 1994, while 5N-OCM, a DC 8-55F, was purchased from Kabo Air Cargo in September 1994; however, it spent most of its time grounded at Ostend and was sold eventually to the British MK Airlines as 9G-MKE in April 1995.

The smell of burned rubber filled the air at Ostend Airport in May 1994 when Captain Giwa touched down 5N-OCL, the flagship of Overnight Cargo Ltd. The B-707-351C's strengthened landing gear has absorbed the aircraft's landing weight since 1967, when it was delivered to Northwest Orient Airlines as N375US.

OKADA AIR

Okada Air was founded in 1983 to become Nigeria's largest private carrier during the decade. The first BAe (BAC) One-Eleven passenger aircraft arrived in September 1983, followed by a single Aérospatiale SE 210 Caravelle 6N three months later, both starting to serve the company's domestic network out of their base at Lagos. 5N-AOQ, a Boeing 707-355C freighter, was introduced in 1984 and became the company's long-serving backbone of cargo charter operations to points in Africa, the Middle East and Europe. Acquiring ten BAC 1-11s by 1990, the short-haul fleet was boosted with a further eight aircraft in 1991 to a total of twenty, creating Africa's largest fleet of this British jet airliner. A Boeing 747-146 painted in the full classic Okada livery was purchased in 1992 and was active as flagship *Lady Cherry* on pilgrimage flights to Jeddah with the meaningful registration 5N-EDO, deriving from the ancient Edo Kingdom of Benin.

5N-AOQ, Okada Air's sole dedicated Boeing 707-355C freighter aircraft, was pictured during one of its last ad hoc cargo charter assignments out of Europe in December 1994. During 1995 the aircraft was ferried to the Jet Support Centre at Manston, UK, to face an uncertain future. Okada Air's tail fin logo portrays an ivory mask, carved during the 16th century in the ancient kingdom of Benin, South Nigeria.

RACE CARGO AIRLINES

As the successor to Rainbow Cargo Airlines founded in 1986, Race Cargo Airlines continued to charter forty-ton-capacity B-707 and DC-8 operators and to maintaining a continuous trading link between West Africa and Europe. Promoting their activities under the 'Fast Cargo Africa' slogan, flights peaked during the winter, before business on this route cyclically slackened after spring. The first airplane to receive a Race Cargo Airlines sticker on the rear fuselage was a Boeing 707-379C, 9G-OLF, of Phoenix Aviation of Coventry, UK, operating out of London–Stansted and Ostend to Accra in late 1991. A year later, a B-707-347C leased to Air Chad by a Greek lessor was released from being grounded at Athens, to be ferried to the Jet Support Centre at Manston, UK to receive Race Cargo Airlines titles and the former rainbow R as fin logo. Though the company has not operated its own aircraft since 1994, their frequent chartering activities continue.

HR-AMA, Boeing B-707-347C, the only freighter that flew on behalf of Race Cargo Airlines in the company's full livery, is flaring over runway 26 of Ostend Airport in March 1993. The pictured aircraft is shown active a few months before its twenty-fifth service anniversary on the pineapple route between Ghana and Belgium.

AIR RWANDA

Société Nationale de Transport Aérien du Rwanda was founded in 1975 with a small fleet operating domestically out of the capital Kigali throughout the mountainous tropical East African highland. Being Africa's most densely populated nation and cultivating coffee and tea as their major export, long-range air transport became inevitable to allow the country's horticultural harvest a world market. In 1979, a former Air France Boeing 707-328C, 9XR-JA, started to haul perishable consignments to the vital Kenyan harbour of Mombasa on the Indian Ocean. It is only 1,100 km to the east, but almost impossible to reach overland. Rwanda's history is marked by the bloody battles for power between the Hutu and Tutsi tribes which escalated during 1994. During these times of unrest, the company's B-707C was sold to a new owner, resuming operations under the name of Rwandair, while during 1995 only a single de Havilland DHC-6 Twin Otter of Air Rwanda served Gisenyi and Kamembe on domestic schedules.

Boeing 707-328C, 9XR-JA *Impala*, of Air Rwanda arrives at Ostend during the winter season of February 1991. The aircraft was bearing a light blue cheatline and titles when it was acquired from Air France in summer 1979, but already features the actual fin logo showing the national flag's white dove, flying over Lake Kivu and some white mountains, symbolizing the Virunga volcano chain. The cheatline design was altered into the national colours during 1987, with the addition of black titles to the fuselage. In 1991 the technical state of *Impala* was evaluated by Lufthansa engineers at Hamburg, who gave the green light for another decade of cargo services. Having operated for more than fourteen years in the colours of Air Rwanda, the aircraft was sold to the new company Rwandair shortly before the outbreak of the civil war in April 1994. The aircraft was one of nine 707-328C passenger/cargo convertibles introduced by Air France between 1965 and 1968, with the pictured one flying the French flag as F-BLCF *Château Grossbois* for more than twelve years between 1967 and 1979.

SOUTH AFRICAN AIRWAYS

The legendary Springbok service to Europe was inaugurated by Avro Yorks during 1945, which were leased from Imperial Airways and linked London, spending more than thirty-two hours in the air on a voyage lasting sixty-eight hours. Eight Douglas DC-3s and seven Douglas DC-4 Skymasters followed after 1946, and the long-haulers routed to London via Nairobi–Khartoum–Cairo and Rome. Four Lockheed L-749 Constellations took over the Springbok services in 1950, until a Comet 1 was leased from BOAC in 1953. This, however, crashed into the Mediterranean after climbing out of Rome on 8 April 1954. Four DC-7Bs restored the piston age again, flying 21-hour one-stop services via Kano, Nigeria to London. During the company's twenty-fifth anniversary, the twenty-one-strong piston liner fleet was enlarged by seven Vickers Viscount turboprops. From 1960, the Springbok has been able to leap to London in a thirteen-hour overnight cruise, achieved with the help of three pure passenger B-707-344s. SAA was forced to rethink its northbound international route network during 1963 when several African nations denied any overflight permission out of political reasons. On their way to Europe, Ilha do Sal on Cape Verde was chosen as an intermediate stop on northbound legs, and the Spanish island Las Palmas served as a southbound station. The early 1990s brought two of the B-747-444 versions, seven Airbus A320-231s as well as a Boeing 767-2B1 (ER), leased from Lineas Aereas de Mocambique. With an open sky spreading out around South Africa since the lifting of sanctions in late 1993, Johannesburg soon strengthened its position as Africa's biggest cargo hub. During 1995, a B-747-244B combi (ZS-SAR) was converted into a freighter by HAECO at Hong Kong and started twice-weekly all-cargo schedules in co-operation with Lufthansa between Frankfurt, Nairobi and Johannesburg, as well as schedules to New York. A second B-747-200F was planned to be acquired in 1996. Four of the increased gross weight Boeing 777-200s, powered by Rolls-Royce engines, were scheduled for delivery by 1997, and options on a further three, as well as for two B-747-444s, are kept open.

The first dedicated freighter of South African Airways to appear in Europe since the presidency of Nelson Mandela was ZS-SDG, named *Koudou*, seen here taxiing away from Schiphol's cargo centre in May 1995. The initial Airbus combi was delivered to SAA in late 1982, mainly being used in a two-class configuration for 263 passengers on high-density shuttles between Johannesburg, Durban and Cape Town. The new political situation generated a rising demand for all-cargo shipments in late 1993 and led to the implementation of the company's only Airbus on long-haul pure cargo routes, until it was joined by the first B-747-244F in late 1995.

SCIBE AIRLIFT ZAIRE – SBZ CARGO

Purchasing two Vickers Viscount 808s from the Sultan of Oman Air Force in 1976, operations were commenced out of the capital's bustling Kinshasa N'Djili Airport under the name of SBZ Cargo. Up to the early 1980s, the turboprop fleet was enlarged by a Lockheed L-100-30 Hercules and two de Havilland Canada DHC-6 Twin Otters, developing the vital African profile that had to include versatile aircraft suited to a country as vast and unpenetrable on the ground as Zaire. The first jet in 1982 was a used convertible Boeing 727-44C combi, which was substituted by two B-727s, series 30 and 89, during 1983/84. To compete with the local cargo and passenger companies, two long-range Boeing 707s were acquired during 1985. Five Fokker F-27s, two series 400M and three series 500, joined in 1986, linked up to thirty domestic points. The capitals of Burundi and Rwanda were served by Twin Otters out of Goma. Beechcraft King Air 200s and Pilatus PC-6 Turbo Porters rounded up the service spectrum during the late 1980s. By the mid-1990s the fleet, now renamed Scibe Airlift, had sold all of its turboprops, operating schedules with only two B-727s and one B-707-329C, having lost its status as the country's largest private carrier to Shabair of Lubumbashi.

After nearly ten years of Central African transport services for Scibe Airlift Zaire, 9Q-CBJ, the company's sole Lockheed L-100-30 Hercules, is seen when parked for several weeks at Brussels–Zaventem Airport in summer 1988. It was undergoing major maintenance and refurbishment before facing its next assignment. Delivered to the South African Safair Freighters with an already Zairean registration in late 1978, 9Q-CBJ was instantly leased to SBZ Cargo/Scibe Airlift, who utilised the versatile high-capacity freighter from most of Zaire's airstrips. Within several weeks in early 1989, the aircraft's ownership rapidly passed through the books of two American companies, until it became the property of the United States government.

SICOTRA AVIATION

Taking over a DC-8-54F of Zaire Cargo in January 1987, 9Q-CSJ was the first freighter operating out of Kinshasa N'Djili Airport for Société International du Commerce et Transport. At the end of that year a former 1966 World Airways B-707-373C joined the fleet. It had previously been flying for Transportes Aereos Portugueses on their long-haul cargo routings to the newly independent colonies of Guinea Bissau, Angola, Mozambique and Cape Verde as CS-TBJ *Lisboa*. Soon after the acquisition of 9Q-CSB in December 1987, Sicotra's non-hush-kitted B-707 could be observed on occasional cargo services to Belgium, becoming the fleet's only aircraft in summer 1988 when their DC-8-54F was sold to Liberia World Airlines as EL-AJQ. In the aftermath of a violent crisis and the evacuation of Belgian and French citizens out of Zaire in September 1991, Sicotra flights to Ostend appeared without the company titles and logo, simply bearing large cargo letters on the front fuselage. During late 1992 the basic livery of the 707 freighter received the highly visible fin and fuselage titles of its new operator, SkyDec Compagnie Aérienne. Since 1995, cargo flights between Zaire and Europe were contracted to sub-chartered, African-registered companies, as well as to a growing number of Ilyushin 76 operators from the CIS.

With titles and logo deleted from 9Q-CSB, Sicotra's only B-707-373C was taxiing towards its take-off position at Ostend, Belgium after a night stop in May 1992. Trying to leave Ostend on the previous day with a valuable load, the southbound flight had to return to its European point of departure due to the denial of an overflight authorisation by an en-route country. In another case a take-off permission was also not granted by Belgian authorities, due to a 14.5 ton payload of new Zairean money. The aircraft was also used to bring President Mobutu's personal valuables out of Zaire into safety, with a load of Mercedes cars flown into Europe to be stored in France during the early 1990s.

SIMBA AIR CARGO

During March 1995, Nairobi-based Simba Air Cargo introduced its sole Boeing 707-336C to the Kenyan perishable export market. It commenced operations by flying three weekly all-cargo services to Amsterdam, and later Ostend in Belgium.

5Y-SIM at Ostend in December 1995. Twenty years ago it was speedbird G-AYLT of British Airways. During the 1980s, the aircraft served with Zairean and Egyptian companies and finally for Air Hong Kong at the end of the decade. Leased to Coventry-based Phoenix Aviation in late 1992 under the Ghanaian registration 9G-TWO, the freighter was mainly used on cargo charters to Africa. It was then purchased by Simba Air Cargo in spring 1995.

TRANS ARABIAN AIR TRANSPORT – TAAT

Starting dedicated air freight services as a small airline with thirty employees, Khartoum-based Trans Arabian Air Transport received its first leased Douglas DC-8-55F (ST-AJD) in 1983. A second DC-8-54F (ST-AJR) doubled the cargo fleet during summer 1985, with both aircraft flying together until 1988. The Jet Traders were replaced by the first Boeing 707-349C (ST-ALK) in September 1988, followed by the second 338C model (ST-ALP) in early 1989. In 1990, TAAT lost two B-707Cs, ST-ALK, and a leased B-707-321C (ST-SAC), which crashed into a mountain near Athens on its first flight for the company, operated by Sudania Air Cargo. Cargo services continued with the remaining ST-ALP, which was sold to the Grumman Aerospace Corporation for a conversion into a E-8C version of the Joint Stars programme in summer 1992. A further two B-707Cs continued the freight work, with ST-AKW being sold to the Sudanese Azza Air in 1994, while ST-ANP and ST-AMF formed the fleet during the mid-1990s. Two Antonov 26 short-range high-wing turboprop freighters with an excellent rear-loading ramp have been leased from Aeroflot since the early 1990s to be used for regional services. A new corporate livery was first introduced on ST-ANP in early 1996.

Trans Arabian Air Transport's first Boeing 707-349C freighter, ST-ALK, sets out to return to Khartoum, Sudan, departing Ostend in late April 1990. The original 1965 freighter of the Flying Tiger Line served for Aer Lingus, Zambia Airways and National Air Charters until joining TAAT in 1988. The aircraft carried the name *Juba*, the disputed southern Sudanese town on the White Nile. Ten weeks after the picture of ST-ALK was taken at Ostend, the freighter's last flight was recorded on 14 July 1990, when its undercarriage collapsed at Khartoum.

TAMPA COLOMBIA

TAMPA – Transportes Aereos Mercantiles Panamericanos SA – was founded in 1973 by L.H.Coulson, an American entrepreneur who settled in Colombia in the 1930s. Directing its operations out of the main office at the Olaya Herrera Airport in Medellín, TAMPA started domestic cargo operations in 1974 with a Douglas DC-6A/B. In 1975 a further DC-6A followed and international operations to Miami were inaugurated, departing Medellín with fresh-cut flowers. The link to Florida generated the local floral produce and the specialisation of the Colombian export market on the perishable sector. During 1980, two leased Boeing 707-320Cs established direct palletised jet cargo services from Medellín (elevation 1,506m) and Bogota (elevation 2,547m) to Miami (elevation 3m). The first was returned to its lessor IAL in 1981 and the second crashed in December 1983 during take-off from Medellín with a failing engine. Immediately substituted by another, four B-707-320Cs were purchased between late 1986 and 1990, shipping Colombian imports from Miami via Baranquilla to Medellín, and via Cali to Bogota. Following the customer demand and the expansion of business in 1989, a weekly transatlantic cargo schedule to Europe was established with a leased Douglas DC-8-63F. A fifth B-707-324C, HK-3604-X, arrived in late 1990, and a couple of DC-8-71F freighters joined in late 1992. At the end of 1993, a last B-707 cargo flight was carried out to Europe, and a DC-10-30CF of World Airways temporarily continued the schedule to Ostend, but the company soon suspended its European activities in early 1994.

Leased from Comtran International Inc in December 1990, HK-3604-X, manufactured in 1967, was TAMPA Colombia's youngest Boeing 707-324C out of a fleet of five and was assigned to carry out European cargo schedules as a successor to the initial DC-8-63F services. Departing Ostend for Gander and Miami as TPA502 during its last summer in June 1993, the freighter achieves a respectable rate of climb due to a low-return payload, cool air temperatures, a strong headwind and an early retracted undercarriage. The combination of the advanced age of the hushkitted JT3D-3B (Q) Pratt & Whitney turbofans and the regular lack of any of the above favourable conditions, which were contributing to an acceptable take-off performance, increasingly produced spectacular flat-out departures at Ostend Airport in the second half of 1993. HK-3604-X was withdrawn from the transatlantic services in late 1993, which closed the chapter of TAMPA cargo operations to Europe with their own aircraft.

Passing the take-off runway's threshold with a ground clearance of less than twenty feet, the Captain of TAMPA Colombia HK-3604-X pulls up the heavy fully-laden Boeing 707-324C into the skies of Ostend in September 1993. Airborne after a run of about 2,200 metres, the freighter levelled out for the last 1,000m of the runway, eventually achieving a positive rate of climb at the end of the airport area. On 25 April 1992, the already twenty-five-year-old, former Continental Airlines jet N17329 lost its number three engine and strut during a take-off, halfway down runway 9R at Miami International Airport. HK-3604-X reportedly had accumulated 54,007 hours and 20,534 cycles when the number three midspar strut fitting broke, but the crew managed to land safely. A few months after this incident, the aircraft resumed flights to Ostend, continuing to bring flowers and to carry home full loads of acetone, spare parts and any kind of general cargo.

WORLD AIR FREIGHT

Seen at Ostend during May 1994 on lease to the Romanian Jaro International was B-707-321C, 5N-TAS. Under ownership of the Irish Omega Air, the aircraft displayed the rather ostentatious titles 'World Air Freight'. A few weeks later in June, exactly the same livery as 5N-TAS was spotted by American photographers on a retired and former Trans World Airlines B-707-131 turbojet, which had been parked in the Californian Mojave desert since 1978.

TUBEL AIR

This Tunisian–Belgian joint venture took up regular cargo services with a wet-leased Russian Aeroflot Ilyushin 76MDK between Monastir International Airport and Ostend in October 1993, mainly hauling textiles from the smallest but economically most successful North African nation among the five states of the Maghreb Union. Tubel Air's trans-Mediterranean link continued until July 1994, when its first aircraft, RA-78825, did not return from an overhaul at Moscow. A second Ilyushin 76MDK, RA-76766, then became listed under Tubel Air ownership; however, this aircraft never undertook regular services or received any other than its Aeroflot colours.

Tubel Air's sole Ilyushin 76MDK, RA-78825, with Arabian titles on the port-side only, arriving at Ostend on its regular morning flight TBR2101 from Monastir. Retaining its basic Aeroflot colours and registration, Tubel Air insisted on having the Tunisian flag painted on the outer engines, and the company logo applied on the fin during the wet-lease charter contract. The Il-76MDK is a special version not often used for civil operations; the MD designation stands for military features, as for example different navigational system and a long-range fuel capacity, while the K is the abbreviation for Kosmos, indicating that cosmonauts and scientists used this aircraft to simulate weightlessness for training and experimental purposes.

AEROLINEAS URUGUAYAS -AUSA-

This Montevideo-based carrier was established in 1990 and was related to the cargo specialist Aero Uruguay, which had operated a B-707-331C freighter since 1978, and after a larger break, a DC-8-55F and a B-707-321C during the late 1980s. CX-BPL was the first and sole jet freighter of Aerolineas Uruguayas, its worldwide cargo charters having begun in the spring of 1990 when Lufthansa Cargo chartered the forty-ton freighter for a number of flights on its South American routings out of Frankfurt. With a low evening sun shedding a warm light on the beautiful freighter at Rhein-Main Airport in March 1990, the former 1967 Trans World Airlines Boeing 707-331C, N5774T, takes on a heavy palletised load for a night flight to Uruguay and Chile with an en-route fuel stop in West Africa.

VARIG BRASIL

Opening services with a Dornier Wal flying-boat in 1927, Otto Ernst Meyer, an expatriate officer of the German Air Force, held a licence to develop a domestic route network out of Porto Alegre throughout the vast southern state of Rio Grande do Sul. In 1941 a fleet of Junkers F13, G24, A-50, J552, and Messerschmitt M20 aeroplanes formed Viacão Aerea Rio-Grandense, better known under its short name VARIG. With Brazil entering World War II together with the Allied nations against Germany, Meyer had to leave his presidential post and Reuben Bertea took over the lead. A restructured fleet policy was putting de Havilland DH Rapides into service, which were operating the first international schedules to Montevideo. Ten Lockheed Electra 10A/Bs were kept until the end of the war in 1945, when a large number of more than thirty C-47 Dakotas and further Curtiss C-46 Commandos expanded the route network way up to the north of the huge Brazilian territory. During the 1950s and 1960s, VARIG changed from a regional airline to South America's largest carrier, successively integrating several national airlines. The first jetliners were introduced in late 1959 with three Rolls-Royce-powered Sud Aviation Caravelle 3s, followed by two Boeing 707-441s. A dozen McDonnell Douglas DC-10-30 widebodies entered service in 1974, with three aircraft being converted into freighters during the late 1980s. The worldwide route system of 1995 included more than thirty international capitals, of which fourteen were in South America, four in the US, three in Asia, and eleven in Europe.

PP-VMT seen rolling the last few metres to its stand at Frankfurt Airport in May 1989. As one of three McDonnell Douglas DC-10-30Fs PP-VMT was VARIG's first passenger DC-10-30, delivered in 1980, to be converted into a dedicated full-freight version in November 1986.